So close to Glory

Warrington Rugby League Football

1919 to 1939

Eddie Fuller and Gary Slater

London League Publications Ltd

So close to Glory
Warrington Rugby League Football Club 1919 to 1939

Front cover photo: Warrington players training at Wembley before the 1933 Challenge Cup Final. Portraits: Bill Shankland and Billy Dingsdale. Back cover: The Prince of Wales meets Arthur 'Candy' Evans before the 1933 Challenge Cup Final and caps won by Jack 'Cod' Miller and Tommy Blinkhorn, with a Warrington rosette from the 1930s (photo: Eddie Fuller). Title page: The traditional Warrington 'Excelsior' club badge, which appeared on the front cover of every Warrington home programme between the wars (courtesy Alan Domville).

A CIP catalogue record for this book is available from the British Library.

Published in March 2008 by:
London League Publications Ltd, P.O. Box 10441, London E14 8WR

ISBN:	978-1903659-37-3
Cover design by:	Stephen McCarthy Graphic Design 46, Clarence Road, London N15 5BB
Layout:	Peter Lush
Printed & bound by:	Biddles Ltd King's Lynn, Great Britain

This book is dedicated to the efforts of the players who have worn the primrose and blue of Warrington with pride, from the birth of the club to the present day. Without them we would have no one to cheer and no one to write about.

Foreword

I signed for Warrington from Rylands in 1937 after playing some trial games for the 'A' team. I was 18 and it was one of the proudest days of my life – and not just because I got a £75 signing-on fee, which I put in the bank.

Warrington was my hometown team and I had been paying 2d to stand in the boys' pen at the Spion Kop end and watch them play. The next season I was running out to play alongside Dave Cotton, Billy Dingsdale, Jack 'Cod' Miller and Jack Arkwright. What a great feeling!

They were a lot older than me. I was just a kid and they were men. Dave Cotton was a brilliant hooker and such a consistent player. He was just as good at the end of his career as he was at the start. Centre Billy Dingsdale was an artist and he was famous for lobbing the ball over opponents' heads to run round them and catch it again. You could never tell what he would do because he was such a fine footballer.

Prop Cod Miller was a real character and one of the reasons why we had such a great camaraderie in the team. Jack Arkwright was big, rough and dirty. He was a good forward, a destructive forward, but I don't know if he would go down too well today.

Also in the dressing room we had Jackie Hamblett, the groundsman, who looked after our every need and was a workaholic.

We tried to train two nights a week, Tuesdays and Thursdays, but nobody said anything if you didn't turn up. I was a toolmaker at Rylands and worked round-the-clock shifts and so couldn't always make it.

I made my debut against Widnes at Wilderspool in August 1939 and I can still remember the team: Billy Belshaw at full-back, Ossie Peake on the right wing, I was right centre, Billy Dingsdale then Izzy Davies, Eli Dixon and Mel de Lloyd at half-back, Eric Welsby, Cotton, Cod Miller, Harry Jones, Ivor Bennett and Bill Chapman.

The following month war broke out and, in 1940, I played in the game against Broughton Rangers at Wilderspool when the Germans dive-bombed Thames Board. I remember it very clearly. I was just getting in the bath and I thought the stand was going to fall in. Nobody expected it. Nobody knew what it was. I don't think we'd had a bomb before. It was terrifying.

Wilderspool was requisitioned in 1941 and so six of us went to Keighley as guest players. One of the Keighley directors, a scrap merchant, lent us a little

Ford 8, but we had to supply our own petrol. I'm not kidding you, I don't know where De Lloyd got the petrol from, but that arrangement lasted for one season. After that we went by train, taxi, hire car, any way we could.

After the war, I played in the match when Brian Bevan made his debut for Warrington. He didn't score that day, but he was fantastic, a one-off. He did his own thing. Attendances of 20,000 were regular and they had ring-side seats around the ground. They wouldn't allow that today either. Wilderspool had bags of atmosphere then and you could hear supporters stamping their feet in the wooden stand.

I had to retire through injury in 1948 and Chris Brockbank, the manager, offered me a place on the staff which I gladly accepted. I was on the staff until 1960, training and coaching, mainly with the 'A' team. I saw a lot of good players come through – Eric Fraser, Jim Challinor, Laurie Gilfedder, Jackie Edwards, Bobby Greenough and Brian Glover all came through the 'A' team.

I've seen, played alongside and coached some magnificent players, from Dave Brown and Billy Dingsdale in the 1930s to Brian Bevan and the cup-winning teams of the 1950s. But I've got particularly fond recollections of Bill Shankland's team who reached two Wembley finals in the 1930s. Shankland was a hard man, a strong tackler and a team leader. When he knocked them down, they felt it.

I am sure you are going to enjoy reading about those happy days.

Fred Higginbottom

Photo: Fred Higginbottom in action for Warrington.

Photographs and illustrations

Introduction

"Those who drink from the well should remember those who dug it."
This Chinese proverb was a favourite saying of Harry Bath, the great Australian forward who played for Warrington from 1948 to 1957, winning two Challenge Cups and two Championships.

The golden age of Warrington Rugby League Football Club ran from 1946 to 1956: from Brian Bevan's first try, against Salford at Wilderspool on 14 September 1946, to the end of the 1955-56 season, when Warrington finished top of the league. During that heady decade, Warrington were crowned champions three times, won the Challenge Cup twice and achieved all manner of records. The period is brilliantly covered in Robert Gate's book *The Great Bev: The rugby league career of Brian Bevan*.

The foundations for that success, however, were laid much earlier, during the two decades between the World Wars. The hard work and forward thinking shown between 1919 and 1939 paid rich dividends – eventually.

Against a backdrop of poverty, economic hardship and mass unemployment, Wilderspool was transformed from little more than a pitch with a fence around it to a magnificent stadium capable of staging a Championship Final or Challenge Cup semi-final. Warrington also developed their fan base so that their record home attendance more than doubled – from 11,000 to 29,000.

The Wire also gained a reputation for signing top-quality Australian players like Bill Shankland and Dave Brown, paving the way for the recruitment of legends like Brian Bevan and Harry Bath in the immediate post-war years.

Bob Anderton, the club secretary, became one of the most respected and knowledgeable officials in the game. Chris Brockbank was appointed team manager as the club moved away from the days when the team was picked by committee. Cumbrian full-back Billy Holding emerged as the greatest goalkicker the club had ever seen. Warrington made their first and second trips to Wembley.

Despite all this, however, these 20 years were also a frustrating time. Warrington did win the Lancashire Cup four times – in 1921-22, 1929-30, 1932-33 and 1937-38 – and the Lancashire League title once, in 1937-38, but the game's major prizes remained tantalisingly out of reach.

Warrington reached three Challenge Cup Finals and three Championship Finals and lost the lot. They also finished second in the league three times. They were always the bridesmaids, but never the bride. They were so close to glory.

Eddie Fuller and Gary Slater

About the authors

Eddie Fuller was the photographic manager at the *Warrington Guardian* from 1972 to 1995 and covered Warrington's Wembley finals in 1974, 1975 and 1990. Now retired, he remains a regular contributor to the Warrington Wolves matchday programme. He is also a multiple award winner and, in 1985, was the British Institute of Professional Photographers' national photographer of the year for his picture of Kevin Moran's sending off in the 1985 FA Cup final between Manchester United and Everton.

Gary Slater was born and bred in Warrington and saw his first Warrington match in 1972 at the age of 10. He was a pupil at Penketh High School and graduated from Imperial College, London, in 1982. He is a former deputy sports editor of the *Warrington Guardian* and *Birmingham Evening Mail* and is currently a senior production journalist and news editor on the *Daily Telegraph* sports desk in London. He, too, has been a regular contributor to the Warrington Wolves matchday programme.

Acknowledgements

So close to Glory has been a labour of love and the authors would like to thank a whole host of people for their help and support. Peter Lush and Dave Farrar of London League Publications Ltd offered good advice when it was needed.

Neil Dowson, of Warrington Wolves, gave encouragement and supplied photographs, as did Mike Parsons, of the *Warrington Guardian*. Warrington supporter Alan Domville read the page proofs and provided historic programme covers.

Stan Lewandowski, of the Warrington Past Players' Association, gave us access to his collection of memorabilia, while rugby league historian Robert Gate was able to supply some elusive facts and figures. Photographer Bob Brough helped with computer technology.

Thanks also to Michael O'Hare for sub-editing, Steve McCarthy for designing the cover, Peter Lush for doing the layout and the staff of Biddles for printing the book.

Eddie Fuller and Gary Slater

Pounds, shillings and pence

Great Britain between the wars was a very different country to today. There was a king on the throne, an empire to run, hardly any television sets and a different currency – Imperial currency. Bizarrely – to modern eyes at least – there were 12 old pennies (12d) in a shilling (1s) and 20 shillings in a pound (£). Currencies in this book are given in old money, which lasted until decimalisation in 1971. Put simply, one old shilling was worth five new pence. For example, Warrington made a profit of £342 18s 7d on the 1918-19 season, which translates to £342 and 93p.

Contents

Full-back Billy Holding kicked a then club record 834 goals for Warrington between 1928 and 1940.

Prologue: 1914 to 1918

The First World War was a time of great hardship and sorrow throughout England, and Warrington and its rugby league football club were no exception. More than 90 players and former players fought for their King and country during the conflict and, tragically, 10 of them made the supreme sacrifice.

That roll of honour was headed by the great Welsh forward George 'Ponty' Thomas who made 385 appearances for the Wire, including four Challenge Cup Finals. Following the outbreak of war in August 1914, Thomas was among the first to enlist and joined the South Lancashire regiment. He remained the larger-than-life figure that supporters knew and reportedly entertained the troops in the trenches by loudly singing *The Yellow Rose of Texas*.

In April 1916, Thomas, who was a private, sent a letter from the Western Front to the Orford Hotel in Warrington for Harry Ashton, the former Warrington captain and secretary. Showing extreme candour and courage, he wrote: "I have had some trying times on the football field and our side usually came out on top but as true as there is a drop of British blood runs through my veins I hope to give the Germans a sound thrashing.

"But if I should fall you can tell the boys I fell fighting like a hero should do for his King and country. We have had a rough time of it and have been constantly harassed by the Germans. Many comrades fell and twice I had narrow escapes. I helped on one occasion to carry my sergeant to a place of safety and bandage him up."

In late June 1916, Thomas was made a Colonel's orderly before, in the early hours of Monday 3 July 1916, he was killed in action on the Somme. An eyewitness reported that he was "blown to pieces" by a German shell. He was just 35 and left a wife and young family living at Walton Road in Stockton Heath.

Australian winger Jim Stuntz, who had scored 13 tries in 19 appearances during the 1909-10 season, was another high-profile casualty. He died on the Somme on 3 May 1917 while serving as a private with the Australian infantry. Stuntz was only the third Australian to play for Warrington and lined up on the opposite wing to Jackie Fish, the club's first superstar.

On the outbreak of war, Fish joined the King's Royal Rifles, the crack regiment of the British Army, and such was his popularity with Warrington fans that many of them signed up for the same unit, which became known as Fish's regiment. Fish won the Aldershot Command Sprint Championship, aged 35, but was invalided out of the services with chest problems shortly afterwards.

Centre or winger Howard Davis was not so fortunate. He was killed in action on the Western Front, aged 27, in July 1915. He had been signed from the Coventry club in 1912 and scored one try in 22 first team appearances before joining the eighth battalion of the Rifle Brigade.

Stand-off Stanley Young also perished. He had joined Warrington from Abertillery in 1913 and formed a fine half-back partnership with scrum-half Syd

Nicholas. Young made 60 appearances in less than two years, scoring two tries, before he signed up for the Manchester Regiment. He was killed by an exploding shell in April 1918, aged 29.

Harry Ashton kept a record of all the Warrington players who served in the War. The others who did not return were Buff Berry, a sterling and plucky forward; James Andrews, who died in Gallipoli; E.J. Burton, a threequarter from the Wigan area; Dalby Newall of the Rifle Brigade; G. Oakes, whose nickname was 'Gosher'; and Alex Brown, a half-back from Salford.

Jimmy Tilley, who had been the full-back when Warrington won the Challenge Cup in 1907, was awarded the Distinguished Conduct Medal in 1916 for "conspicuous gallantry". Details of his heroism were published in the *London Gazette* as follows: "He, with three others, rescued a buried man from a dug-out under very heavy shell fire. Six shells fell in the farm and one within five yards of the party. On another occasion, with a small party, he attacked the enemy and advanced 100 yards down their trench. As bomb sergeant at that time he was continuously harassing the enemy." Tilley's luck ran out in 1918 when he suffered facial wounds and lost his right eye.

Arthur Naylor, who was a forward in the Warrington teams who won the Challenge Cup in 1905 and 1907, was shot by a sniper in 1917, with the bullet passing through his ear, neck and back. "But I am glad to tell you," he wrote in a letter home, "that I am improving. The doctors say that I am a very lucky man to be living. I am in a military hospital, and am being well looked after. Remember me to all old friends."

Following the popular belief that the war would be "all over by Christmas" the Rugby Football League – or Northern Union as it was known at the time – had tried to carry on as normal in the 1914-15 season. The league campaign kicked off on the first Saturday in September and finished on the last Saturday in April, leaving May, June, July and August free for cricket.

But it became increasingly difficult to carry on as normal, especially after 25 players had volunteered for the army. A Warrington versus Wigan midweek game had to be postponed because Warrington had so many players on Government work that they could not raise a team.

There was also a Keystone Kops type moment on Saturday 16 January 1915 when efforts by the Warrington Fire Brigade to remove water from the Wilderspool pitch before a match against Leeds failed and the referee said he would leave it to the clubs to decide what to do. Both teams decided to play but the referee stopped the game after 65 minutes because the conditions were so bad. However, the result, a 3-3 draw, was allowed to stand.

Competitive games were suspended at the end of the 1914-15 season and Warrington decided not to take part in the series of friendly games that were arranged for 1915-16 and so some of their best players – notably full-back Ben Jolley and centre Jim Tranter – played for Runcorn instead.

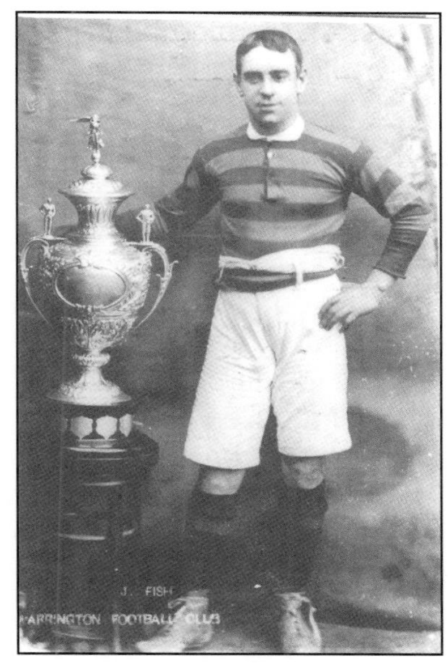

Left: Winger Jack Fish played in four Challenge Cup Finals for Warrington. Right: Welsh forward George 'Ponty' Thomas sang *The yellow rose of Texas* in the trenches to entertain the troops.

With no sign of the war ending, Warrington quickly realised the error of their ways and re-entered the fray the following season, although finding suitable players was still a major problem. To illustrate the point; for the opening game, at Leigh on Saturday 2 September 1916, they played a stranger at full-back, whose surname was Wheeler, who was picked up at the local railway station.

Leigh were in a much better position. They had 20 players, all anxious to play and play for nothing. Of the 13 who were selected, 10 had worked in the pit that morning and, according to the match report, two were still covered in coal dust. St Helens, on the other hand, were in dire straits and when they visited Wilderspool, Warrington paid their expenses. In total, Warrington used 52 players during the 1916-17 season, including one, intriguingly, called Cullen.

It was a similar story in the 1917-18 season when 45 players were used. Again, every club was facing similar difficulties. After experiencing travel problems, Swinton arrived at Wilderspool for a match on Saturday, 17 November 1917 with only four players and so they borrowed six Warrington reserves and played with 10 men. The kick-off had to be delayed while all the problems were sorted out and so the match, which Warrington won 33-0, finished in semi-darkness. It was Warrington's biggest win of the season and helped them to finish 10th out of the 22 teams in the Merit Table, which had replaced the Championship for the duration of the War, with a 58.06 percent success rate from their 31 matches.

Before a new season could begin, Warrington lost one of their leading lights on 14 September with the death aged 58 of Ted Warren, the former club captain, secretary and president. His obituary was front-page news in the

Warrington Guardian. Although he was born in Braunston in Northamptonshire, and spent his early career with the Padgate rugby club, he had been Warrington's delegate at the George Hotel in Huddersfield on Thursday 29 August 1895, when 21 northern clubs resigned from the Rugby Football Union to form the Northern Rugby Football Union. Warren, incidentally, was also a founding member of the Commercial Travellers' Association and a prominent Freemason, associated with a slate company in the town.

The First World War – "the war to end all wars" as it was optimistically known – finally came to an end at 11am on Armistice Day: 11 November 1918. The country then embarked upon the job of building a land fit for heroes which, for Warrington's men at least, meant watching their beloved Wirepullers in action.

The Northern Union met on 8 December to lift the ban on competitive matches and decided that players could receive broken-time payments not exceeding 10 shillings per match. This was a major step backwards from the unrestricted professionalism of the pre-war days and would prove unsustainable.

Away from rugby league, Warrington again elected a Conservative MP, Mr Harold Smith, who had first won the seat in 1910, at the general election on 14 December. This was the first election at which all men over the age of 21 and all women over the age of 30 were eligible to vote.

No doubt that was one topic of conversation at Atkinson's café on 18 December when the Warrington committee treated many of their old players to a hot-pot supper, although they were probably more concerned about the limit on their pay. Four friendlies were arranged in December and January, with Widnes visiting Wilderspool on Boxing Day 1918 in the first.

It was like old times with a crowd of 5,000 turning out to see Warrington win 3-0 thanks to a try from winger Jack Jolley who kicked the ball over the full-back's head and then won the race for the touchdown. Unfortunately, the second friendly, at home to St Helens on New Year's Day 1919, had to be abandoned because Wilderspool was flooded.

A visit to Widnes followed on 4 January. The game attracted fewer than 1,000 supporters and Warrington, whose team was severely depleted, had to borrow three players, two from the Runcorn club and one from the hosts. One of the newcomers, 'Ponty' Lewis, a former Runcorn threequarter, was Warrington's best player as they lost 5-0.

Seven days later, while the process of war demobilisation continued, Leigh visited Wilderspool. Warrington won 11-8, scoring all their points in the first half, including two tries from winger Syd Grounds. Grounds had been discovered playing for Warrington butchers against St Helens butchers in a match at Wilderspool in 1913. He was a fine sprinter but, unfortunately, because of his job, he found it almost impossible to take Saturday afternoons off to play for Warrington.

By now, an interim Lancashire League had been arranged to run from mid-January to mid-May. Warrington's campaign began badly with a 13-3 defeat at

Widnes, watched by a crowd of just 1,500, and they finished the match with just 11 men following injuries to stand-off William Potter and centre L. Rogerson.

Defeats at Wigan and St Helens quickly followed but, at least, in early February there was some good news for the players: at another historic meeting at the George Hotel in Huddersfield the clubs voted to return to unrestricted professionalism. Some clubs pushed for a maximum wage of £1 per match but the majority, including Warrington, who were represented by Edmund Osborne, the chairman of the committee, voted to return to the pre-war arrangements.

Warrington were drawn at St Helens in the first round of the Lancashire Cup on 5 April and the game attracted 9,000 - Knowsley Road's biggest crowd for years - including 2,000 from Warrington. Warrington won the toss, decided to play with the strong wind at their backs in the first half and led 5-3 at the break. It was not a big enough advantage and St Helens ran out worthy winners 11-5.

At least Warrington enjoyed a memorable Easter, with three home victories in four days. Salford visited Wilderspool on Good Friday, with Warrington winning 11-0 in front of 8,000 supporters. All the points were scored in the first half. Twenty-four hours later, Rochdale Hornets were in town for a match that attracted a crowd of 9,000. Again, Warrington scored all their points in the first half with two magnificent penalty goals from winger Jack Jolley sealing a 4-0 victory. Next up were St Helens Recreation on Easter Monday when a last-minute try from centre Jim Tranter rounded off a 9-2 win. The Easter games proved that Warrington was still a hot-bed of rugby league and the gate receipts totalled an impressive £608, although the Government immediately took £166/9/0 in the unpopular entertainments tax.

The season ended in May with nomination papers for club officials being released. Harry Ashton was nominated for the post of president while Bob Anderton was put forward for the post of secretary.

The annual general meeting was held at Cairo Street School on Thursday 29 May 1919. Ashton was the unanimous choice for club president, but Anderton faced a ballot against a Mr W. Bibby, which he won by 65 votes to 28. Tom Pemberton, who had been the honorary treasurer since the 1881-82 season, on the amalgamation of the Warrington and Padgate clubs, presented his final set of accounts. He was stepping down after 37 years in the post. Warrington had made a profit of £342/18/7 on the season, despite paying out £404/17/6 in entertainments tax.

Interestingly, two final Lancashire League tables were produced: one that included every game played and an official one where fixtures were only included if the clubs had played each other home and away. Warrington finished third in the official table, with Wigan fourth, while the positions were reversed in the unofficial version. Obviously, Warrington supporters regarded the official table as the true measure of a team's worth.

Jim Tranter

Left: Captain of Lancashire versus Yorkshire in the 1919-20 season. Right: Tranter's hook - getting to grips with an unsuspecting opponent.

Left: Kicking the ball upfield. Right: Rival mascots shake hands before the Challenge Cup second round replay against Leigh at Wilderspool in March 1921.

1. 1919-20: A new beginning

Club president: Harry Ashton. Club captain: Ben Jolley.

After four years of war, there was a great sense of anticipation before the start of the 1919-20 season. There was also a feeling that a new era was beginning. Bob Anderton, who had served in the South Lancashire regiment during the conflict, started work as honorary secretary at the age of 31 and over the next 50 years he would become the greatest and most energetic administrator in the club's history. Famous for his dapper appearance and blue and white polka-dot dicky bow, he was also a keen compiler of scrapbooks and a prolific writer on rugby league - without his efforts, books like this would not be possible.

One of his first actions was to revamp and relaunch the official programme, which before the war had been little more than a team sheet. Priced 1d, the new-look programme contained club notes, the teams, fixtures, league tables, photographs and free-to-enter competitions and soon became very popular with supporters and generated much-needed income. The programmes also featured the Warrington Football Club Excelsior badge on the front. The badge, of course, had its origins in the decision of the fledgling Warrington club to amalgamate with the Padgate Excelsior club in 1881.

Rugby league lost many players and supporters during the Great War and also lost one of its founder clubs, Runcorn, who went out of existence in 1916. Their sad demise, however, proved to be good news for Warrington who signed one of their best players, forward Alf Peacock, in August 1919. Peacock received a signing-on fee of £7/10/0 which he repaid many times over during the next 10 years as he made 367 appearances. Peacock, who wore a skull cap to cover up his balding head, became Warrington's first specialist hooker. Before he signed, scrums were formed quickly and whoever arrived in the middle of the front row first would attempt to win the ball for his team. Peacock changed all that.

He made his debut in the opening game of the 1919-20 season which, in a radical and controversial break with tradition, began in August, two weeks earlier than usual, because Great Britain would be touring Australia and New Zealand the following summer. The clubs had also been reminded that it was compulsory for the players to wear numbers on their jerseys. There had been some problems with this during the previous Lancashire League season.

The clubs could not wait to get started. Apart from anything else, they needed the money. The players were professional – even though they only received winning pay or losing pay, and the occasional signing-on fee – and needed to be paid. Fortunately, there was a post-war boom in the economy and Warrington took in a record amount of gate money during the season: £5,722. Their biggest pay day came on Saturday 3 January 1920 when a record 16,000 crowd packed into Wilderspool for the visit of Huddersfield, the league leaders. The crowd was made up of 14,700 who paid at the turnstiles, including many from Widnes, and 1,300 members and complimentary ticket holders. The turnstiles opened at 1.00pm and 10,000 were in the ground by 2.00pm. To add to the tension, the Huddersfield team arrived late, meaning that the 2.30pm kick-off had to be put back 15 minutes.

The pitch quickly became a mudbath, yet Warrington played exceptionally well for the first 20 minutes and took the lead when Billy Cunliffe scored the opening try after the Warrington pack wheeled the scrum over the line. Ben Jolley's kick hit the crossbar and bounced out. Huddersfield, however, were the bigger, stronger side and Stanley Moorhouse soon scored an equalising try. Warrington were then hit by injuries to centre Jack Jolley and scrum-half Jim Daintith. Jolley left the field for treatment, but bravely returned to the fray before receiving another injury and had to retire for good. Daintith, at least, was able to continue, although Warrington withdrew Tom Cunliffe from the pack to play at half-back with Daintith switching to the threequarters. Huddersfield made the most of Warrington's misfortunes, adding three more tries to win 14-3.

Huddersfield went on to finish top of the table while Warrington could only finish 10th out of the 25 teams, having collected 53.33 percent of the available points. This calculation was necessary because the teams did not all play the same number of games. Some, like Huddersfield, played 34 games, Warrington played 30 times while Leigh and St Helens Recs only had 28 fixtures.

In what would today be considered a remarkable transfer, Warrington signed a player from Manchester United FC. Joe Haywood had been a half-back in association football - a midfield player in modern terms - with United and had made 48 first team appearances. Haywood had started playing football with the Sankey club before joining Hindley Central in Wigan. From there, he signed for United in May 1913 for a fee of £50 and made rapid progress at Old Trafford, playing in 14 First Division games in the 1913-14 season.

While serving as a soldier in France, however, he started to play rugby and enjoyed it. After the war, aged 26, he started training with Warrington and played very well in the pre-season practice matches. So, on Saturday 30 August he played for Warrington's 'A' team as A.N. Other on the right wing against Swinton Park. Warrington won 21-3 and Haywood continued to impress. He signed professional forms on Wednesday 3 September and the committee had no hesitation in selecting him for his full first-team debut the following Saturday; against Widnes at Wilderspool. Haywood was named on the left wing and such was the excitement that supporters were urged to arrive early and have the correct money available because there were only a limited number of turnstiles.

The reporter from the *Warrington Guardian* could not contain his excitement. "Chief interest will be centred on the appearance in the home team of Joe Haywood, the Manchester United Association half-back. For several weeks Haywood has shown capital form in the practice games and the improvement has become so marked that the committee had no hesitation in placing him on the team for this afternoon's match. Haywood developed with the Sankey Association Club and subsequently migrated to Wigan. His stay there was not long for the Manchester United Club found in Haywood a 'jewel in the rough' and it was not long before he graduated into first-class league, playing with United for four seasons. He is 26 years of age, and has a splendid turn of speed, and will train into a player much above the ordinary."

The game attracted a crowd of 8,000, who paid gate receipts of £370, but Widnes, not for the first time, and certainly not for the last, spoiled the party with a comfortable 14-0 victory. Two days later, Haywood made his second appearance, at Huddersfield, but fractured his collarbone in the last minute while making a tackle, an injury that would keep him out for almost three months. He returned to action in December and finished the season with three tries in 22 appearances and a regular slot on the right wing. All the while, he was still on United's transfer list, although by May 1920 his fee had been reduced to £20. Haywood's Warrington career quickly fizzled out, however, and he was eventually transferred to Widnes before returning to his first love, football, as a non-League player. He later became a licensee in Lymm, although his son, Ron, was a physiotherapist with Warrington in the 1950s.

Warrington's campaign, in a gloomy foretaste of what was to follow, was undermined by injuries. Ben Jolley, the Warrington full-back, captain and goalkicker for the 1919-20 season, did not escape the injury curse. He suffered a broken right leg – a fracture just below the knee – at home to Dewsbury in January, an injury that ended his season and almost certainly cost him a place on the Great Britain tour of Australia and New Zealand that summer. No wonder he looks so miserable in the cigarette cards of the time. Jolley had been in magnificent form and scored the only try of his 282-game Warrington career in the 15-4 victory at Wigan in December. Warrington were already down to 12 men, following Alf Peacock's sending off for a wild kick, when the full-back – or 'custodian', as the position was known – intervened. Collecting a kick downfield, Jolley paused for a moment and the Wigan team expected him to return the kick. Jolley, however, spotted a gap in the Wigan ranks and sprinted over in the corner. Even the Wigan supporters cheered.

In Jolley's absence, Arthur Fowles made his debut at full-back and quickly earned the nickname 'Farmer' because of his style of play. He was slow and deliberate but could hoof the ball huge distances and kick goals from the halfway line with hardly any effort. Fowles was also an international water polo player, but was suspended by the Amateur Swimming Association because he was paid for playing rugby league. The establishment had still not forgiven rugby league for having the temerity to start paying its players broken-time money (compensation for missing work) in 1895, 25 years earlier.

Warrington's home game against Broughton Rangers on 31 January was a benefit match for two pre-war stalwarts, forward Arthur Naylor and utility player Ernie Jordan, and all the proceeds went to them. Each player was presented with a cheque for £102/1/2. One of their leading pre-war team-mates, Ernie Brookes, aged 35, was drafted into the team at the last minute after George

Walker was taken ill on his way to the match. Warrington still won easily, 18-2.

As usual, the Challenge Cup campaign generated a lot of excitement, especially after Warrington were drawn at home to a junior team, Askham-in-Furness, in the first round. The result was never really in doubt, but a crowd of 8,000 still turned out to see the action and they were rewarded with Joe Haywood's first try for the club. He kicked the ball over the full-back's head, dribbled it to the line and then touched down to set Warrington on their way to a 9-0 victory. Warrington were drawn at Oldham in the second round and the match attracted a crowd of 19,000. Warrington's pack was one of the best in Lancashire and had been described as the 'terrible six' but, once again, they were let down by their back division and lost 9-0.

Two of the Warrington forwards, Billy Cunliffe and Arthur Skelhorn, played in the various trial matches to select the Lions squad and were chosen for the tour to Australia and New Zealand. Each was presented with suits, worth £50 apiece, and £25 in cash by Harry Ashton, the club president, as a reward for their selection. News of Skelhorn's call-up was even recorded in the St James' Church parish magazine as follows: "We extend our congratulations to Mr A. Skelhorn, who has been chosen to go out with the representative English NU rugby team to Australia. Mr Skelhorn is a regular attendant at St James's and we take it as an additional honour to the Church." St James's, of course, is the imposing sandstone church 100 yards from Wilderspool.

The tourists left home in April and on the first leg of their journey, from Tilbury to Marseilles, a fellow passenger was David Lloyd George, the Prime Minister. He was introduced to each member of the party, shaking hands and wishing them well for the tour. Cunliffe and Skelhorn both made their full international debuts in the front row in the third test at the Royal Agricultural Ground in Sydney on 10 July. Against all expectations, Britain won 23-13, but Australia had already won the first two tests to reclaim the Ashes.

Buoyed by the spectator boom, Warrington made a profit of £303 on the season, despite having paid £1,050 in entertainments tax, and promptly signed two promising players from the Wigan Highfield club – scrum-half Frank McNulty and winger Bert Cartwright – to beef up the back division. They had already completed the signings of two threequarters from junior clubs – William Brockbank from Barrow St George's and Tom Nicholls from Pemberton Rovers and hopes were high that the following season would be better.

The war, of course, was still in everyone's minds. At the end of March, Wilderspool held a crowd of 6,000 for a match to raise money for the Discharged Sailors' and Soldiers' Association. The teams were captained by Huddersfield's Harold Wagstaff, the doyen of centres, and Chic Johnson, the Widnes and international forward. Johnson's team won 13-8. The teams were as follows:

Johnson's team: Garforth (Halifax), Johnson (Widnes), Davies (Warrington), Seeling (Wigan), Stacey (Halifax), Mooney (Leigh), Finnerty (Oldham), Cartwright, Coffey (Leigh), Ramsdale (Wigan), Fitzsimmons (Rochdale), Corcoran (Widnes), Pollitt (Swinton).

Wagstaff's team: Fowles (Warrington), Haywood (Warrington), Wagstaff (Huddersfield), Redmond (Widnes), Waywell (Warrington), Rogers (Huddersfield), Reid (Widnes), T. Cunliffe, W Cunliffe, Fearnley, Robinson, Skelhorn (all Warrington), Higgins (Widnes).

Warrington also commissioned a roll of honour from a local artist, a Mrs Box, bearing the names of all the players who had perished in the war. It remained in the committee room or boardroom for more than 60 years until the main stand was destroyed by fire in April 1982 and it was lost forever.

A local hero: Chris Vose

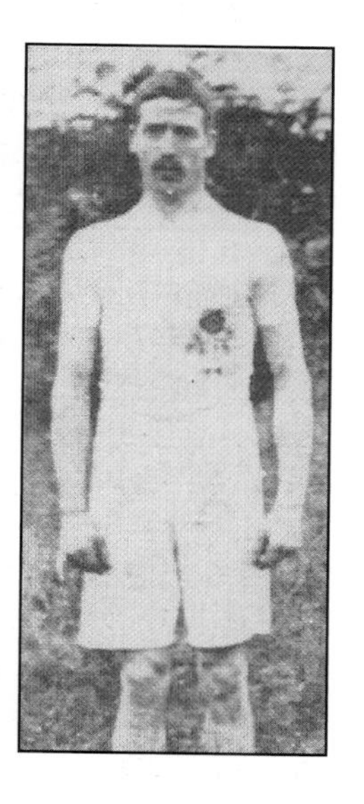

Chris Vose was Warrington's first Olympian, representing Great Britain in the men's individual cross country in the 1920 Games in the Belgian city of Antwerp. He also captained the men's cross country team and, for many years, was the Lancashire captain.

Vose, who was born on 27 January 1887, was a leading member of Warrington Athletic Club in their most successful period and was an outstanding runner. As a young man he took part in races around the Wilderspool pitch before matches, which provided valuable speed work for the challenges ahead.

He first achieved national prominence in 1911 when he won the West Lancashire and Northern cross country titles and led Warrington AC to their first victory in the West Lancashire event. He then finished third in the English Championships as did the Warrington team. Those performances saw him selected for England.

Warrington's best year as a team was 1913 when they won the West Lancashire title, with Vose as the individual winner, and took the Northern crown for the first time. In the English Championships, Warrington and Vose both finished runners-up.

Then came the war years, just at a time when Vose was reaching his prime but, in 1920, he again led Warrington to victory in the West Lancashire and Northern championships and returned to the England team.

At the Olympics, of course, he was up against the best athletes in the world and could only finish 19th in the individual cross-country behind the legendary Finnish runner Paavo Nurmi who took the gold medal. By now his international career was drawing to a close but he continued to shine at club level. In 1922, Warrington again won the West Lancashire title with Vose taking the individual honour. The following year, aged 35, he helped Warrington to retain the title.

When his running career ended Vose maintained a close interest in Warrington AC, of which he was later made a life member, and in 1961 an annual Chris Vose road race was instigated in his honour. Vose died, aged 83, in Grappenhall in August 1970.

Team effort: The players who raised money for the Discharged Sailors' and Soldiers' Association with a match at Wilderspool in March 1920. Left to right, back row, Joe Cartwright, John Corcoran, Dick Ramsdale, Arthur Fowles, Arthur Skelhorn, Harry Robinson, Bowen. Middle: Chris Redmond, Jim Finnerty, Clem Garforth, Jim Pollitt, Harold Wagstaff, Councillor Robert Henshall (the Mayor of Warrington), Albert 'Chic' Johnson, Charlie Seeling senior, Cyril Stacey, Tommy Cunliffe, Jack Higgins. Front: Davies, Joe Haywood, Johnny Rogers, Jim Fearnley, Jack Waywell, Fred Coffey, Walter Mooney, Bill Reid.

Left: Alf Peacock was Warrington's first specialist hooker and made 367 appearances from 1919 to 1929, claiming two Lancashire Cup winners' medals.
Centre: Prop-forward Billy Cunliffe was selected for the Northern Union (Great Britain) tour of Australia and New Zealand in 1920.
Right: Warrington captain Ben Jolley missed out on the Northern Union tour after breaking a leg against Dewsbury in January.

2. 1920-21: To win or not to win

Club president: Harry Ashton. Club captain: Ben Jolley.

If some stories are to be believed then Saturday 12 March 1921 is one of the most shameful days in the long and proud history of Warrington Rugby League Football Club. For it is alleged that the players decided not to win a Challenge Cup second round tie at Leigh. Rather, they would accept a draw so that they could get paid extra for the replay at Wilderspool.

With the scores locked at 10-10 and time rapidly running out, Warrington were awarded a penalty which Ben Jolley, their full-back, captain and goalkicker, lined up to take. As he made his preparations, centre Jim Tranter and loose-forward Arthur Skelhorn came over to speak to him, to discuss, according to rumour, the merits of settling for a replay. The kick was missed, the match ended in a draw and a replay was required.

Yet it seems grossly unfair and unreasonable to suggest that the kick was missed deliberately and that these men, three of the greatest players in the club's history, acted improperly. Ben Jolley was a fine goalkicker but, in front of a crowd of 21,000 spectators, this was a high-pressure kick and not a formality. Jim Tranter was another highly respected figure in the game and had captained Lancashire against Yorkshire the previous season.

Tranter, who was 6 feet 1 inch tall and weighed 14 stones, had long arms and had perfected a type of tackle that became known far and wide as 'Tranter's hook'. These days such a challenge would be classed as a high tackle and penalised, because he became adept at allowing an opponent to almost pass him before whipping an arm across his neck to bring his progress to a shuddering halt. Many an unsuspecting player thought he had beaten Tranter only to end up catapulted backwards. In fairness to Tranter, though, who was from the Longford area of the town, he only used his 'hook' against opponents who had been dishing out punishment themselves without being penalised by the referee. Off the field, he was a gentleman, teetotaller and model professional.

Skelhorn, too, was an honourable man. He even refused to play or watch rugby league on Good Friday because of his strong religious beliefs and was respected and admired for his stance. He would have been horrified at the thought of Warrington playing regularly on a Sunday as they do now.

These three then were not the kind of players you would normally expect to be involved in such shameless shenanigans. The allegations against them, however, were well known and are recorded in the book that was written by Bill Garvin, a former Warrington director, to mark the club's centenary in 1979.

Of course, other factors may have come into play. Draws are relatively rare in rugby league and so the players traditionally received winning pay for a draw away from home and losing pay for a draw at home. If Ben Jolley did deliberately miss the kick he and his team-mates would not have lost money.

They would still have received winning pay. It is also perhaps true to say that the club would have been happier with a draw than a victory because of the money a replay would generate. Indeed, the rematch four days later attracted a crowd of 19,400 to Wilderspool.

Having already beaten Leigh home and away in the league, Warrington began the replay as favourites but, in a major upset, they lost 8-3 with Emlyn Thomas, the Leigh centre, playing the game of his life. Leigh, who only finished 20th in the league, went on to win the cup for the first time in their history. If Warrington did decide to give Leigh a second chance in their second-round tie they were certainly punished for their arrogance.

Coincidentally, the replay marked the 155th and final appearance in a Warrington shirt of one of their finest scrum-halves, Jim 'Shint' Daintith, aged 34, who had played in the 1913 Challenge Cup Final team that had lost 9-5 to Huddersfield's famous 'Team of all the Talents'. Daintith had earned his nickname 'Shint' because of his prowess at the game of shinty, which is rather like hockey but is played with curved sticks and taller goalposts. Daintith, a lifelong Warringtonian, had played shinty as a boy when he and his friends used to cut branches from willow trees to use as sticks and collect bungs from the brewery rubbish tip to use as balls. He had signed for Warrington from the London and North West Railways amateur rugby league club in the 1907-08 season. The majority of his first-team appearances were as a scrum-half, but he also proved his versatility by featuring as a stand-off and full-back.

Warrington's first round tie in 1921 had also gone to a replay after a 5-5 draw at Hull that ended with a pitch invasion by some of the 15,000-strong crowd. The referee, M.C. Denham of Broughton, had to be escorted to the pavilion by Warrington players but was still kicked and had his jacket torn.

Joseph Barton, the Warrington prop who had been sent off and was standing on the sidelines, was knocked senseless by a fan with a heavy stick while Tommy Cunliffe received a serious blow in the face. An inquiry was held and Hull were ordered to post notices at the ground warning spectators against disorderly behaviour.

Warrington won the rematch 16-5 thanks to a hat-trick of tries from winger Bob Bradbury, a new signing from Rochdale Hornets. Bradbury was not a great player but he was fast and whenever he was presented with a clear run to the line there was no catching him. The replay, which kicked off at 5.30pm on Wednesday 2 March, certainly captured the imagination of the people of Warrington and attracted a record crowd of 21,206 to Wilderspool, with record gate receipts of £1,090.

That was the second record crowd of the season at Wilderspool as October's Lancashire Cup tie against St Helens Recs had been watched by 19,992 supporters. On that occasion, the crowd were entertained by the Stockton Heath

Military Band before kick-off. The match also marked the return to the side of Billy Cunliffe and Arthur Skelhorn following the Great Britain tour of Australia and New Zealand. The pair had already been the guests of honour at a welcome home tea party for 50 people at the Kings Café in Bridge Street – where the JJB Sports shop can now be found. This was followed by a trip to the Royal Court Theatre in Rylands Street to see *The Lilac Domino*, a musical comedy. The Royal Court Theatre, incidentally, was demolished in 1960 and replaced by a supermarket that later became 'Poll Tax House'. But, despite the team bonding, Warrington failed to take their chances against St Helens Recs and lost 9-5.

Bob Bradbury was not the only new signing. Stand-off Jack Prescott, a former Wigan player, was signed from Hull Kingston Rovers for what proved to be a bargain £100 before the season started. He even inspired a limerick in a competition in the programme. Here are three of the better entries, but remember this was 1920, long before the issues of sexism and political correctness were invented.

Since watching our half-back, Jack Prescott
I've a fluttering under my waistcoat.
From pride of my heart,
He has ousted the tart,
Now she's selling the ring and the bed-cot.

Our half-back is classed as A1,
The Froggies would say he's tres bon -
Though little, he's wise,
A terror for his size,
McNulty is second to none.

Bill Cunliffe is full of his banter,
Though he can't run as fast as Jim Tranter,
He might for a lark
Get a match on with Clarke
I'll bet he would win in a canter.

Warrington's first home match of 1921, against Huddersfield on 8 January, was attended by three knights: Sir Harold Smith, the Conservative MP for Warrington; Sir Gilbert Greenall, of the famous brewing family; and Sir Peter Rylands; the industrialist. Sir Harold and Sir Peter had both been knighted in the New Year honours. All three were accompanied by their wives. Sir Harold was given the honour of kicking off the match and was pictured doing so in the following week's *Warrington Guardian*. Warrington still lost 5-0, in front of a 14,000 crowd.

Another side of Warrington life was on view at the end of the month, however, when a soup kitchen was opened on Monday 31 January, at the Buckley Street Methodist Church to help combat the hunger caused by unemployment. On the first day, 240 children from 50 families were fed. By the following Friday, as word spread through the town, that figure had risen to 546 children from 135 families.

In February, Warrington lost one of their former playing heroes with the death, aged 58, of James Jolley (no relation to Ben Jolley), who had been a key member of the first Warrington team to win a trophy, the South West Lancashire Cup in 1886. Jolley had started his career as a back before becoming a forward and being capped by Lancashire. One of his best performances had been in 1881 when his drop-goal from near the halfway line had beaten a highly rated Wakefield Trinity team at Wilderspool.

Also in February, George Formby senior, the famous Lancashire comedian, died in Stockton Heath aged 45 of tuberculosis, leaving a widow and seven children including, of course, George Formby junior.

Warrington Athletic Club held their five-mile championship at Wilderspool before the league match against Halifax on Saturday 5 March. Inevitably, Chris Vose won the race in a time of 26 minutes and one second and was 20 yards clear of the runner-up.

The following month Wilderspool staged a benefit match for Jack Birchall, a Warrington 'A' team player who had suffered a broken neck in a match at Widnes. The teams were captained by two Great Britain internationals, Warrington's Arthur Skelhorn and Huddersfield's Harold Wagstaff, and the match attracted a crowd of 5,000. Skelhorn's team won 21-13, scoring five tries. The money was used to set Birchall up in business as a milk dealer.

During the season, Warrington also paid an undisclosed sum of money to a man named Colonel Lyon to buy the land on which the main stand was built. Previously, the land had only been rented. So despite Warrington taking in record gate receipts of £11,713 during the season – the post-war boom was still continuing – they finished the campaign by making a profit of just £2/13/11.

Warrington finished second to Wigan in the Lancashire League and 13th in the full league table. It was now 14 years since they had won a trophy.

Left: Man of principle: Arthur Skelhorn refused to play or even watch rugby league on Good Friday because of his strong religious beliefs.

Below right: Winger Bob Bradbury scored a hat-trick of tries to send Hull crashing out of the Challenge Cup.

Below left: Scrum-half Frank McNulty was a terror for his size.

Above: Warrington Captain Ben Jolley (right) shakes hands with Jack 'Tot' Wallace before the Challenge Cup tie against St Helens Recs in February 1926. The referee is the Reverend Frank Chambers of Dewsbury. Warrington won 17-12 after a magnificent game. The gate receipts were £1,260 – a then record for a cup tie at Wilderspool.

3. 1921-22: At last, the Lancashire Cup

Club president: Edmund Osborne. Club captain: Jack Prescott.

Warrington had already lifted the Challenge Cup twice – in 1905 and 1907 – but had still not won the Lancashire Cup. Under new captain Jack Prescott, however, they finally put that right in the 1921-22 season.

Warrington made a poor start to the campaign, losing four of their opening five league games, but enjoyed the luck of the draw in the first round of the Lancashire Cup when they were awarded a bye.

Home victories over St Helens Recs and Leigh quickly followed to put Warrington into the final against Oldham at The Cliff, which was then the home of Broughton Rangers but would later become Manchester United's training ground.

1921 Lancashire Cup Final

Oldham versus Warrington at The Cliff, Broughton on 3 December 1921.
Attendance: 18,000

The crowd included 5,000 Warrington supporters and was treated to a roller-coaster match.

Warrington suffered a major blow before the kick-off when Great Britain international Arthur Skelhorn withdrew from the side because of a leg injury. He did not want to jeopardise the team's chances. Jim 'Scuddy' Fearnley took over at loose-forward. More injury drama would follow.

Warrington started well and took a 2-0 lead after eight minutes with a penalty from full-back Ben Jolley but then, approaching the half hour mark, disaster struck. Centre Charlie Collins suffered a dislocated shoulder and had to leave the field, leaving Warrington to play with 12 men for 53 minutes.

Tom Cunliffe was pulled out of the pack to reinforce the backs and Warrington managed to cling on to their slender advantage until half-time, before Oldham drew level with a penalty goal from Reg Farrar.

The odds had shifted Oldham's way, but Warrington winger Bob Bradbury charged down a Farrar kick and hacked the ball forward to score a superb, opportunist try in the corner. Jolley missed the conversion but later added a second penalty goal to make the score 7-2.

Undaunted, Oldham launched another series of attacks and Joe Ferguson, their veteran forward, scored a try near the posts from what looked like a forward pass to make the score 7-5 with the kick to come. All the pressure was now on Farrar and he cracked, sending his shot wide and handing the cup to Warrington.

Warrington's homecoming was particularly moving and noisy. The approaches to Central Station were packed and, after a parade through the town, the crowd moved on to Wilderspool to give the team a tumultuous welcome.

The following week a celebration dinner was held at Kings Café in Bridge Street. After the meal and various speeches, there was musical entertainment and amusing monologues. Captain Jack Prescott also performed his impersonation of George Formby senior.

The Lancashire Cup win must have been particularly satisfying for one of the club's new committee members, Danny Isherwood, the former Warrington centre who had made 297 appearances for the first team between 1896 and 1908, but never won the competition.

Even before the Lancashire Cup run, Warrington had made it a season to remember by becoming the first club side to beat the 1921-22 Kangaroos. Ten teams had already tried and failed by the time Warrington beat Australia 8-5 at Wilderspool with Ben Jolley, who kicked four penalty goals, again the hero.

The match attracted a crowd of 16,000 who paid record ground receipts of £1,700. During the latter stages, however, the gates were thrown open and at least 2,000 more supporters packed in to see a thrilling victory.

Before the match, like New Zealand do today with their haka, Australia performed their war cry:

Wallee Mullara Choomooroo ting-al,
Nah! Nah! Nah! Nah!
Canai, Barrang, Warrang, Warrang,
Yallah! Yallah! Yallah! Yallah!
Ah; Jaleeba booga boorooloong,
Yarnah meei, meei, meei,
Neeyarra, Weyarra, Jaleeba, Cahwoon,
Cooeewah, Cooeewah, warr, wooh

Translated:

We are a race of fighters, descended from the war gods
Beware! Beware! Beware! Beware!
Where we fight there will be great bloodshed;
Go! Go! Go! Go!
We are powerful but merciful, are you
friends? Good, good,
The Kangaroo is dangerous when at bay;
Come on, Come on, to death.

Australia returned to Wilderspool in December and lost again, this time 8-6 to a Lancashire side containing three Warrington players – Billy Cunliffe, Arthur Skelhorn and Jim Tranter – who were each paid £3 for their efforts, thanks to the new rates of pay on offer for representative games. Great Britain appearances were worth £7, England appearances £5 and county matches earned the player £3.

Left: Jack the lad - Warrington captain Jack Prescott performed impressions of George Formby senior, the well-known comedian. (Courtesy Stan Lewandowski)
Right: Young gun - Frank Williams signed for Warrington in October 1921.

Cunliffe and Skelhorn played in all three tests against the Australians with Skelhorn producing one of the finest displays of his career in the third and decisive match at Salford – on a ground ankle deep in mud – to help Great Britain win 6-0 and reclaim the Ashes.

Despite having two Great Britain forwards, Warrington's form dipped alarmingly after Christmas and they lost 15 of the last 23 games as younger players were given their chance in the team. Included in that dreadful run was a 55-3 defeat at Wigan, one of the heaviest defeats in the club's history. Wigan, the best team in the land then, ran in 13 tries. Their backs were irresistible and Warrington were no match for them. A crowd of 15,000 was present at the kick-off but that grew to 20,000 by half-time as latecomers arrived.

The next home game, against St Helens Recs, drew a crowd of just 2,500, but that was more due to vile weather than the supporters being disillusioned. Warrington won 8-5 with tries from Billy Cunliffe and 'Scuddy' Fearnley.

In the middle of February, Warrington gained revenge for that thrashing at Wigan by winning the return fixture at Wilderspool 10-6 thanks to two second-half tries from centre Jim Tranter. His second try was particularly memorable as he intercepted a pass from Jim Sullivan before scoring. Nine thousand people paid to see the match with another 1,000 admitted for free at half-time.

In the build-up to the Challenge Cup first-round tie at Dewsbury, 16 Warrington players visited Northwich Brine Baths for rest and relaxation, but the salty water did not work any magic. Jolley pulled out of the team through injury half an hour before kick-off while captain Jim Tranter was hurt after 20 minutes. Although in pain, he played on for an hour. But his bravery was to no avail. Warrington lost 13-2 and, after that, lost seven of the final 10 league games.

The only highlight during that period was a home game against Rochdale Hornets in March, which was billed as a benefit match for former scrum-half Jim 'Shint' Daintith and for the widow of George Thomas, the legendary Welsh forward who had lost his life on the Somme. Both parties received £127/8/11.

Jim Tranter finished the season as the leading try scorer with 15. Ben Jolley became the first Warrington to player to kick 50 goals in a season, a feat which was much more difficult in those days because rugby balls were bigger and heavier and the pitches were often waterlogged and muddy.

Warrington's finances were not as impressive. They lost £1,572 on the year, taking their debts to £2,500. Economic conditions were difficult for all businesses, however, and unemployment was growing. So from Saturday 15 October 1921 until the end of the season the committee agreed to make 350 tickets per match available to the unemployed free of charge.

At least the 'A' team offered hope for the future, with promising youngsters like stand-off Stan Wheatley, centre Frank Mason, winger Eddie Makin, scrum-half Freddie Ryder, winger Arthur Hassall and second-row Frank Williams.

Williams had been discovered playing for Cheshire Lines in the Warrington Works competition and signed for £25 in October 1921. He would go on to become Warrington's highest scoring forward with 87 tries in 352 appearances. As well as being an outstanding second-row, Williams was also a very versatile player. In one match at Broughton in January 1924, for example, the Warrington full-back was injured just before half-time so Williams moved out of the pack to take his place for the rest of the match.

Warrington made another interesting signing in December 1921, winger Elliot Harris, the son of the legendary Warrington winger of the same name. Harris senior made 172 appearances from 1898 to 1906, scoring 59 tries and playing in two Challenge Cup Finals. "If this youngster turns out to be as good as his father, then we shall have reason to congratulate ourselves on the capture," wrote Bob Anderton in the programme. Harris senior was one of the 'Aristocratic Four' of Jack Fish, Danny Isherwood, George Dickenson and Elliot Harris whose threequarter play was described as "poetry in motion". Sadly, Harris junior was not as gifted. He played for the 'A' team but never for the first team.

On 13 October 1921, women's football was played at Wilderspool, with Dick, Kerr's Ladies team (named after a factory in Preston), beat a team from Farnworth 11-0. A crowd of 4,000 enjoyed the game, raising funds for the Warrington branch of the Royal British Legion.

The sport's AGM was held from 30 June to 3 July at Keswick where a major change was made with the renaming of the governing body. The Northern Union days were over and the Northern Rugby Football League was born. The last link with the Rugby Football Union had been broken.

4. 1922-23: The bone cracked... people fainted

Club president: Edmund Osborne. Club captain: Billy Cunliffe.

All injuries are painful and unpleasant, but some are more painful and more unpleasant than others, as the Warrington supporters who watched the 'A' team game on 18 November 1922 discovered to their cost. George Lloyd, one of Warrington's 'A' team players, had a leg broken in two places. Most of the spectators in the ground heard the bone crack and two or three people fainted. It was an experience they – and he – would never forget and summed up the bad luck the club was suffering at the time. Warrington had already lost another centre, Frank Mason, with fractured collar-bone at Broughton on the opening day of the season, an injury that kept him out of action for two months.

Warrington began their defence of the Lancashire Cup with victories over Broughton Rangers and St Helens to earn a home semi-final against arch rivals Wigan. Warrington went into the match with high hopes, until stand-off George Walker suffered a leg injury after 15 minutes that was to rule him out for the rest of the season. Wigan were already leading 2-0 thanks to a Jim Sullivan penalty when Walker departed and Warrington were forced to reorganise their team. Second-row forward Tommy Cunliffe was withdrawn from the pack and put in the threequarters while centre Jim Tranter moved to stand-off to replace the unfortunate Walker. Warrington, however, took the game to Wigan and, when Tranter was obstructed, Ben Jolley kicked the resulting penalty to make the half-time score 2-2. It was too good to last and second-half tries from winger Tom Coles and centre Tommy Howley gave Wigan an 8-2 victory and they went on to beat Leigh by 20-2 in the final at Salford.

Warrington's Challenge Cup campaign was equally ill-fated. They were drawn at home to Halifax in the first round, but had to be content with a 3-3 draw after centre Jim Tranter was sent off by the referee, Reverend Frank Chambers, for allegedly striking an opponent. Tranter was banned for two matches and so missed the replay which was scheduled for the following Monday but had to be postponed because of a heavy snowstorm.

When the replay finally did take place a week later, on Monday 26 February, the pitch was in a deplorable state and part of the match was played in semi-darkness. On one occasion the teams even struggled to find the ball which had become lost in the straw around the playing area.

Cumbrian Bob Scott, who had signed for Warrington from his hometown club Aspatria for £350 the previous December, had one of his best games for the club. Playing at full-back, he fielded the ball in all sorts of positions and his catching and handling skills were almost uncanny, but it was all to no avail. Halifax adapted to the difficult conditions far better and won 16-3.

Warrington's league form was even more depressing with more defeats, 19, than victories, 17, for a 15th place finish and a 47.22 per cent success rate. Not surprisingly perhaps, the fans began to show their frustration. The referee, Mr

Left: Warrington signed veteran Widnes and former Great Britain forward Albert 'Chic' Johnson in January 1923.

Hestford of Broughton, stopped the game against Oldham at Wilderspool in December 10 minutes from time after receiving abuse from the crowd. The supporters were furious that the referee had disallowed what they thought was a perfectly good try by Dickie Blackburn, the Warrington winger.

The referee spoke to Billy Cunliffe, the Warrington captain, and Bob Anderton, the Warrington secretary, who, in turn, tried to reason with the crowd. Several minutes elapsed before play resumed and, even then, the referee blew for full time four minutes early, condemning Warrington to an 8-3 defeat. The Rugby League management committee held an inquiry into the affair and decided that it did not constitute a serious matter. Warrington were told to issue a warning to fans in the programme and the committee also regretted that Mr Hestford ended the match four minutes early.

Also in December, Warrington put full-back Ben Jolley, the former captain, on the transfer list with a price tag of £750, a huge sum of money at the time. Jolley complained to the Rugby League management committee and had the fee cut to £200 but there were still no takers and Jolley did not play again that season.

Warrington did make two important signings ahead of the Challenge Cup transfer deadline in January when they recruited experienced centre Chris Redmond and former Great Britain forward Albert 'Chic' Johnson from Widnes. By then, however, the rot had set in.

The club also made a financial loss of £357 on the year's activities. In summary, it was a season to forget, particularly so for Billy Cunliffe, Warrington's Great Britain prop-forward, who had been appointed captain.

Billy and his younger brother Tommy had joined Warrington within a few months of each other in 1914 from the Pemberton Rovers amateur club and both made their first-team debuts in the 1914-15 season. Billy was a specialist prop-forward while Tommy was at home anywhere in the pack and there was plenty of sibling rivalry between the pair.

They were also a couple of characters and the late Jackie Hamblett, who worked on the Warrington ground staff for 60 years, loved to tell the story of how they tried to outdo each other by being first in the bath after a game to get the benefit of the hottest and cleanest water. On one occasion, they both jumped into the bath together only to discover the water was too hot. They both let out a yell and jumped out again, but Tommy, determined not to be beaten, ran back into the dressing room, put his socks back on and returned to the bath undaunted.

When Hamblett first arrived at Wilderspool in 1920, as a lad of 16, he used to make himself useful by doing all sorts of jobs, such as helping out with the kit. The players soon realised he was not being paid and Billy and Tommy Cunliffe, together with Jim Tranter, formed a deputation on his behalf to insist that the committee put the matter right. They emerged from the boardroom to announce to Hamblett that he was now on the staff and was to be paid 4/6d for first-team duties and 3/0d for 'A' team duties.

Billy, who was 5 feet 10 inches tall and weighed 14 stones 10 pounds, was the type of forward who could play the game to suit the occasion and his opponents soon learned to appreciate this. He could be skilful or he could be rough, tough and ruthless. He played in 35 of Warrington's 41 matches during his season as captain while Tommy made 38 appearances, but they had precious little to show for their efforts.

Away from rugby league, Sir Harold Smith had stood down as the Conservative MP for Warrington at the general election in November 1922 and been replaced by another Conservative, the dashing Captain Alex Reid DFC. Captain Reid had been educated at Harrow School and Cambridge University and won the Distinguished Flying Cross while serving with the Royal Flying Corps during the war. One of his most ardent supporters was Lady Greenall who was the first person to vote when the polling station in Stockton Heath opened. Captain Reid received 15,394 votes to beat the Labour Party candidate, James Gregory, a councillor from Leigh, by 1,824 votes in a two-horse race. The turnout was a staggering 85 per cent.

Left: Tommy Cunliffe made 324 appearances for the Wire, scoring 48 tries.
Right: Wilderspool legend Jack Hamblett worked on the groundstaff for 60 years.

Left: Stand-off George Walker was injured in the Lancashire Cup semi-final against Wigan.
Right: Utility back Tom Mannion made 20 appearances during the 1922-23 season after signing from Barrow.

5. 1923-24: Ticket to salvation

Club president: Fair Barber. Club captain: Jim Tranter.

Supporters of horse racing will be fully familiar with the Cambridgeshire Stakes, a nine-furlong handicap race for three-year-olds and upwards that is run every October at Newmarket and which, with the Cesarewitch, forms part of the Autumn Double. In 1923, the winning horse was called Verdict, but – more than 180 miles away – the real winners were Warrington Rugby League Football Club.

Warrington had started the 1923-24 season with major financial problems, including an overdraft of £1,173 at the bank, which is more than £1 million in today's prices. They finished the campaign in credit to the tune of £188. The remarkable turnaround in the club's fortunes was due, almost entirely, to a sweepstake the club held on the Cambridgeshire Stakes. Club officials, committeemen and supporters sold tickets for one shilling each and, after a slow start, the sweepstake grew and grew in popularity. One supporter by the name of Jack Knowles sold 2,800 tickets on his own and, at the final count, more than 44,000 tickets were sold and the sweep made a profit of £1,676/5/7. Warrington's financial worries were over – at a gallop. Warrington's supporters also formed a Supporters' Club with the stated objective of "supporting in every possible way the best interests of the club".

From the start of the season, the committee had known that the team was not good enough and so made six important signings – with mixed results. Scrum-half Freddie Ryder was signed from Cadishead on 18 August 1923. He and his club were given £20 each and it would prove to be money well spent. For two years, for example, from 20 September 1924 until 25 September 1926, he made 86 consecutive appearances.

Another scrum-half, Jerry Donovan, was signed from Oldham in November for £300, but did not quite live up to expectations and was sold to Keighley for £65 two years later. Donovan, in fact, is best remembered for the fact that he often used to head the ball like a football player.

Arthur Childs, a rugby union winger from South Wales, was recruited after two trial games, one for the 'A' team against Widnes 'A' at Wilderspool in October and one for the first team at Oldham in November. On both occasions he was given the pseudonym Fletcher, Bob Anderton's middle name.

Arthur Smith, a 21-year-old centre, also joined in November and arrived with an impressive sporting pedigree. Smith, who was 5 feet 9 inches and 13 stone, was the son of Thomas Smith who had helped Tottenham Hotspur win the FA Cup for the first time in 1901.

Rhys Rees, a centre from Hull Kingston Rovers, and Ned Catterall, a goalkicking centre from Dewsbury, were also added to strengthen the squad. At the end of September, full-back Ben Jolley, the former captain, returned to the fold for the first time since the previous November. He played for Warrington 'A' against the Manchester and District League at Wilderspool and more than 3,000 supporters turned out to watch his comeback. Two weeks later, he was back in the first team.

In the first round of the Lancashire Cup, Warrington defeated Barrow 15-2 to earn a home draw against Widnes. That match ended in a 6-6 draw and the replay at Naughton Park finished 5-5 and so a second replay, at a neutral venue, was required. Wigan's Central Park was chosen and, on 5 November, Warrington eventually won 13-2 with tries from wingers Dickie Blackburn and Eddie Makin and right centre Jim Tranter. Ben Jolley and left centre Chris Redmond, the former Widnes player, kicked a goal each. Makin, incidentally, was very quick. He was also a member of Warrington Athletic Club and had enjoyed a successful summer on the track, winning a string of races across the north of England. In February, he was selected for special training ahead of the 1924 Olympic Games in Paris by a meeting of the Northern Counties Association Olympic Committee.

Warrington, however, were well beaten, 19-7, in the semi-final at Swinton in front of a 14,000 crowd despite a fine display from the forwards, with Billy Cunliffe, in particular, showing international form.

The defeat at Swinton began a sequence of six in a row. Results were getting worse before they got better. However, Warrington ended 1923 on a high note when they beat Batley 19-0 at Wilderspool. Batley were second in the league, Warrington were 22nd.

There had been a similar upset in the general election on 6 December when Warrington had mirrored the country and switched from blue to red for the first time. Captain Reid, the sitting Conservative MP, lost his seat to the Labour Party's Mr Charles Dukes, a trade union official, by 670 votes.

Warrington's Challenge Cup campaign got off to a bright start with a 46-3 victory over the Cumberland junior club Dalton at Wilderspool which was followed by a 7-5 win at York. Hopes of further progress were abruptly ended with a 34-7 defeat in front of a 9,100 crowd at Barrow in the next round when everything went wrong and Warrington lost by eight tries to one.

Prop-forward Arthur Skelhorn had suffered a broken collarbone at Wigan seven days earlier, an injury that ended his season and his hopes of making a second Great Britain tour to Australia and New Zealand. Full-back Ben Jolley also missed the match following the death of his wife. Second-row forward Tommy Cunliffe was sent off in the second half after a clash with Barnes, the Barrow loose-forward, who was also dismissed.

Warrington's league form was even worse than the previous year. They finished 20th in the full table, with 16 wins and 20 defeats for a success rate of just 44.44 per cent, but at least – thanks to the sweep on the Cambridgeshire – the club was back in the black at the bank.

Hooker Alf Peacock again proved his ability and durability by playing in 43 of Warrington's 44 matches and being picked for a Great Britain trial match. Unfortunately, he just missed out on selection but his front-row partner Billy

Cunliffe was named, making him the first Warrington player to make two tours of Australia and New Zealand, having made the trip in 1920.

As before, it would be an expensive business. The Rugby League Council would provide a straw hat and a blazer. Cunliffe had to supply the rest of his kit himself and, according to the Warrington programme, that included a cabin trunk, two suits, two sets of pyjamas, plenty of collars, handkerchiefs, socks, two pairs of boots, overcoats (heavy and light), brushes and shaving tackle. All told, that would cost him in the region of £50.

Accompanying Cunliffe on the voyage was Edmund Osborne, Warrington's representative on the Rugby League Council and on the Lancashire County Committee, who was appointed joint manager of the party. Osborne was proving to be an effective administrator and, that March, his revised laws of the game had been discussed and agreed by the Council.

After Warrington's home game against Hunslet in April, Osborne was presented with a gold watch by the club as a token of their esteem while Cunliffe, who was still only 26, was presented with a wallet containing £20 in cash to help him on his way. The pair set sail from Tilbury on board the P&O liner SS Moldavia a few days later. During the voyage, all 26 players were weighed and Cunliffe, at 14 stone 8 pounds, was the heaviest member of the group. No wonder he was such an effective scrummager.

Cunliffe played in all three tests against Australia as Great Britain retained the Ashes won two years earlier. Britain won the first test, at the Sydney Cricket Ground, on 23 June by the impressive scoreline of 22-3 in front of a crowd of 50,005. The following day, also in Sydney, another event occurred which would have a huge impact on the Warrington club and the game of rugby league. A baby boy was born in Waverley, a district in the eastern suburbs. His name was Brian Bevan and, between 1946 and 1964, he would score a world record 796 tries, including an amazing 740 for Warrington.

Left: Winger Dickie Blackburn scored 16 tries in the 1923-24 season. Right: Jim 'Scuddy' Fearnley made 204 appearances between 1911 and 1924, scoring 39 tries and one drop-goal.

Left: Stand-off M. Hanley made three appearances for the first team, all in October 1922. Right: Full-back A. Wright made 22 appearances in 1922 and 1923, kicking three goals.

6. 1924-25: Farewell to Arthur Skelhorn

Club president: Fair Barber. Club captains: Arthur Skelhorn and Jim Tranter.

Before the start of every season Warrington held trial matches to assess and, hopefully, recruit the best of the local talent. The trial matches before the 1924-25 season were somewhat out of the ordinary, however, because Wilderspool was flooded after a period of heavy rain and so the games were staged on pitches at nearby Chester Road. Still, they unearthed a real gem of a player in stand-off Arthur Frowen, who was promptly signed by the club and went on to make 183 appearances for the first team over the next eight years.

Frowen was an all-round sportsman. He had been born in Atherton before his family moved to South Wales where he played football in the Second Division of the Welsh League. He also tried his hand at rugby union and played in a trial match for the Welsh team in his first season. Next, he helped Nuneaton win the Midlands Rugby Cup for the first time in their history and played for Warwickshire in the rugby union County Championship before joining Warrington at the age of 24.

He made 29 appearances as a stand-off during the 1924-25 season, but it was not until March 1926, when he was switched to the full-back role, that he found his best position where he became a ferocious tackler.

Warrington offered 'A' team trials to various likely lads every season. This year, the club ran the rule over four full-backs, 13 threequarters, six half-backs and 16 forwards. Most of them, of course, were not up to scratch, although Warrington did sign at least eight players during the season, including prop-forward Bill Harrop, from Devonport Services RUFC, full-back Harry Lees, from Oldham RUFC and centre Jack Green. Second-row forward W.H. Leyland and centre Norman Abbott, both from Wigan Old Boys RUFC, centre Charlie Stowell, from Warrington Rangers, and Nuneaton centre or full-back Tom Gabriel also agreed terms.

Warrington also signed winger Bill Stockley from Pemberton Rovers. His transfer, however, proved to be anything but straightforward because after he had put pen to paper with Warrington, he also signed on the dotted line for Wigan and the Rugby Football League was forced to investigate. Stockley was suspended for three games for his conduct while Wigan were fined one guinea [£1/1/0] for signing a player who was not on his club's transfer list.

After all that, Stockley made history on his first appearance for Warrington, against Bradford Northern at Wilderspool on Saturday 4 October 1924, when he became the first player to score a hat-trick of tries on his debut for the club. It proved to be a false dawn, however, because he only scored one more try for the first team and, made just 13 appearances before joining Dewsbury. Surprisingly, perhaps, after his earlier brush with authority, Stockley became one of the leading grade one referees after the Second World War.

It was also around this time that Warrington offered an 'A' team trial to a young lad from St Helens. He did not quite make the grade but, a generation later, his son became one of the greatest players the game had ever seen. The father's name was James Murphy. His son was Alexander James Murphy, better known as Alex.

Warrington beat Wigan 9-0 in front of 9,000 fans in their first home league match of the 1924-25 season, but nobody was fooled. Warrington had not impressed against a Wigan team who were still waiting for their big-money signings from South Africa and Australia to arrive.

Featherstone Rovers were the next visitors to Wilderspool and it was their first visit to the ground after only being admitted to the game's professional ranks at the start of the 1921-22 season. Again the match attracted a 9,000 crowd and again Warrington won, this time 25-8.

The Warrington forwards produced a magnificent performance at Leigh in the first round of the Lancashire Cup to engineer an 8-0 victory in front of 14,000 fans, 4,000 of whom had made the journey from Warrington. But Warrington lost 15-5 at St Helens in the next round.

The following week, the people of Warrington were going to the polls again for the third general election in three years. Captain Reid, won the seat back again, beating the sitting Labour MP, Charles Dukes, by 1,537 votes. "Naturally I would have been better pleased if I had won," said Dukes, "but I hope we can be good sports even though we lost."

November also started badly for Warrington when they were thrashed 44-4 at Wigan where the famous Welsh full-back Jim Sullivan scored a try and kicked seven goals. Warrington lost right wing Dickie Blackburn through injury and had to withdraw second-row forward Jim Tranter, a former centre, from the pack to complete the backline, which certainly did not help matters.

At the end of the month Warrington signed a third player from Nuneaton, prop-forward Harry Whitcombe, who had been suspended by the Rugby Football Union in 1923 and had not played since. Whitcombe's 'crime' had been to offer to play for another Midlands rugby union club if they found him a job. The RFU had declared him professional and so he could no longer play their game.

Christmas brought a mixed bag of results. Warrington beat Widnes on Christmas Day, lost at Rochdale Hornets on Boxing Day and travelled to Keighley on 27 December for their third match in as many days. Lawkholme Lane was a sea of mud and the match probably should not have started, but it did, in front of 2,000 hardy spectators. Some of the players soon became so covered in mud as to be unrecognisable and, at one stage, no fewer than five players were unable to play on as they tried to get mud out of their eyes. In the final quarter, the captains decided that enough was enough and that the game should be abandoned, but because an hour had been played the result stood. Warrington won 12-0.

The return at Wilderspool in January attracted a crowd of 7,000 who gave Frank Renton, the veteran referee from Hunslet, a ringing cheer when he ran on to the field. Renton, aged 57, had long been regarded as the doyen of referees and, as such, was highly respected.

Warrington beat Bradford Northern 11-3 in the first round of the Challenge Cup, but were drawn away to Oldham in the second round. Jim Tranter, who had been appointed captain in November following the resignation of Arthur Skelhorn, was full of confidence: "You must know," he told the *Warrington Guardian*, "that Warrington have one of the greatest reputations in England as cup fighters. What Warrington did at Wheater's Field, Broughton in 1907 and at The Cliff, Broughton in 1921 when we won the Northern Union and Lancashire Cups respectively, I feel positive that we shall do again. You see we always rally our special efforts against sides sanguine of the result."

Warrington went into the game without winger Dickie Blackburn, who had flu, and Arthur Skelhorn, who had a damaged shoulder, and lost a gruelling contest 12-2. Despite the result, the forwards had produced another heroic effort.

The season was all but over because Warrington had no realistic chance of reaching the top four and with it a Championship play-off place, but there was still one major highlight to come: the benefit match for Arthur Skelhorn and Jim Tranter. They had chosen the game against Huddersfield, still known as the Team of all Talents, on Saturday 21 March. A crowd of 11,000 turned out to honour the pair, who had made more than 500 first-team appearances between them, and paid gate receipts of £460, all of which went to their benefit fund, as did a half-time collection that raised £50.

Warrington were inspired and produced their best performance of the season, winning 23-11, with Skelhorn and Tranter playing major parts. Tranter created the second try with an elusive run that was the prelude to some slick passing between half-a-dozen pairs of hands for stand-off Bill Siddall to cross near the posts. Skelhorn, meanwhile, scored Warrington's fifth and final try on what would turn out to be his 259th and final first-team appearance. It was his 49th try for the club, a remarkable figure for a forward. Tranter and Skelhorn were later each presented with cheques for £312/13/0.

Skelhorn subsequently resigned as a playing member of the club in September 1925 to concentrate on his new job as the licensee of the Hawthorn Hotel in Orford Lane, a post he would hold for the next six years until his death, aged just 45, of bronchial pneumonia, in April 1931.

After the horrors of the previous year, 1924-25 was a season of considerable progress and they ended up ninth in the final table. Nonetheless, veteran prop-forward Billy Cunliffe was the only Warrington player to gain representative honours – he played once for England and twice for Lancashire – but there was a feeling of better things to come and so the committee decided to extend the main stand. Additional 40 feet bays were to be added at each end to seat an

Left: Ready for battle: Rival captains Jim Tranter and Huddersfield's Harold Wagstaff pose for a picture before kick-off at Wilderspool in January 1921.

Below: A ticket for Arthur Skelhorn and Jim Tranter's benefit match in March 1925. Note that the ticket spells Skelhorn's name wrong by adding a final e.

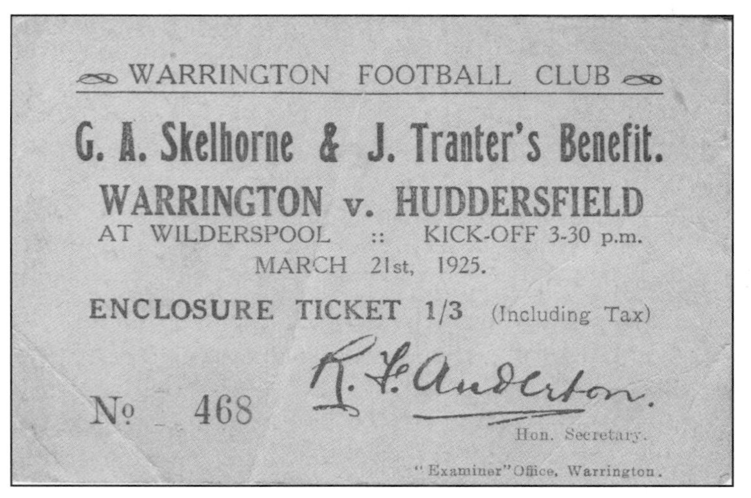

WARRINGTON FOOTBALL CLUB

G. A. Skelhorne & J. Tranter's Benefit.

WARRINGTON v. HUDDERSFIELD

AT WILDERSPOOL :: KICK-OFF 3-30 p.m.

MARCH 21st, 1925.

ENCLOSURE TICKET 1/3 (Including Tax)

№ 468 R. F. Anderton.

Hon. Secretary.

"Examiner" Office, Warrington.

extra 600 supporters and a loan of £700 was secured from the Rugby Football League to help finance the project.

Away from rugby league, at the end of June, winger Billy 'Fanny' Roberts showed his sprinting ability when he competed in the Lancashire County Championship 100 yards race at Manchester United's Old Trafford ground. He finished second in a time of 10.24 seconds, missing out on the title by a foot. Clearly, he had pace to burn.

A local hero: Steve Donoghue

Steve Donoghue is something of a forgotten hero now, even in his hometown, but in the 1920s he was the most famous jockey in the land and his record of riding three consecutive Derby winners and four in five years has still not been broken.

In all, he won the Derby six times – in 1915, 1917, 1921, 1922, 1923 and 1925 – and was Champion Jockey on 10 occasions. When his days as a jockey were over, he became a trainer and registered his own racing colours – primrose and blue hoops – in tribute to the Wire.

But it is as a jockey that he is best remembered. On two occasions, in 1915 on Pommern and in 1917 on Gay Crusader, he completed the Triple Crown by winning the Two Thousand Guineas, the Derby and the St Leger. He also rode Brown Jack, his favourite horse, to an unprecedented six consecutive wins in the Queen Alexandra Stakes at Royal Ascot. After the sixth victory, it took horse and rider 20 minutes to reach the winner's enclosure because of the size and passion of the crowd.

Donoghue also rode The Tetrarch, an enormous two-year-old colt that raced in 1913 and was said to be the fastest horse ever ridden in England.

In his 1974 biography *Steve*, journalist Michael Seth-Smith put Donoghue's success down to "perfect hands". He explained: "No jockey has ever been blessed with the gift of hands as perfect as Steve's – hands which instilled confidence into every thoroughbred by the most delicate and gentle touch. It was claimed that Steve could ride and master the most fractious horse with no more than cotton thread as reins. Certainly the magic of his hands was such that on one occasion doctors X-rayed them in the hope of discovering some quality not possessed by other mortals."

Warrington is not the first town you would pick as being the birthplace of one of the greatest jockeys who ever lived, but it was. Steve was born at 51 Aikin Street, a terraced house in the Bewsey/Whitecross area of Warrington, not far from where the Mad Hatter pub can now be found, on 8 November 1884.

Aged six, he went to school at the St Mary's Roman Catholic School in Buttermarket Street. He struggled academically and often played truant but was a natural horseman. His first contact with horses and ponies was at Arpley Meadows where he would jump on their backs and ride round gleefully.

In 1899, aged 14, he became a stable lad with John Porter, the most famous trainer in England, at his yard at Kingsclere, near Newbury, and so began a long and difficult apprenticeship. Steve would have to ride in France, Ireland and South Africa before truly being recognised as a great jockey in England.

Yet when success finally arrived, it was sustained and spectacular and cries of "Come on Steve" echoed across racecourses throughout the country. Steve was also generous to a fault and never forgot his hometown. After his sixth Derby triumph in 1925, for example, he treated 800 pupils from his former St Mary's School to a celebration party.

At a dinner in his honour at the Dorchester Hotel in London in April 1938, his friend and fellow jockey, Gordon Richardson, paid him the following tribute: "No jockey and few men in our time have enjoyed the popularity of Steve Donoghue, but believe me, however popular he may have been with the public, he was still more popular among us in the weighing-room, for he helped the least, the last and the poorest of us."

Donoghue died, aged 60, after suffering a heart attack at his home in London on 23 March 1945 but was buried in Warrington Cemetery. More than 200 wreaths were laid beside the grave. A hospital bed at Warrington Infirmary was endowed in his memory.

A year after his death a memorial stone was erected in Warrington Cemetery. It took the form of a seven feet high headstone, on three bases, made in grey granite. A racehorse head, modelled on a photograph of Brown Jack, was carved at the top.

Donoghue was in the news again in November 2007 when the race to be Champion Jockey between Seb Sanders and Jamie Spencer ended in a dead heat. It was the first time the title had been shared since 1923 when Donoghue and Charlie Elliott both rode 89 winners. Donoghue had been Champion Jockey outright for the previous nine seasons.

Donoghue was in the news again in November 2007 when the race to be Champion Jockey between Seb Sanders and Jamie Spencer ended in a dead heat. It was the first time the title had been shared since 1923 when Donoghue and Charlie Elliott both rode 89 winners. Donoghue had been Champion Jockey outright for the previous nine seasons.

Oldham 12 Warrington 2 in the Challenge Cup

Warrington's second round Challenge Cup tie in the mud at Watersheddings in February 1925 ended in defeat after a gruelling contest.

Scrum-half Freddie Ryder makes a break at against Batley at Wilderspool in August 1925 when the pitch was still enclosed by a wooden fence.

Shall we dance? The Warrington team line up during the 1924-25 season. Left to right: Jim Tranter, Arthur Skelhorn, W.H. Leyland, Frank Williams, Arthur Childs, Billy Cunliffe, Tommy Cunliffe, Alf Peacock, Dickie Blackburn, Billy 'Fanny' Roberts, Ben Jolley and Arthur Frowen

7. 1925-26: The General Strike

Club president: Fair Barber. Club captains: Ben Jolley and Fred Ryder.

From the turn of the century onwards, Warrington established a reputation as a formidable cup team. In fact, by the mid-1920s they had already appeared in five Challenge Cup finals and two Lancashire Cup finals, but their league form had been consistently disappointing. Finally, in the 1925-26 season, they put that right.

After nine games, Warrington were top of the table with eight wins and one defeat and a success rate of 88.88 per cent. They had scored 164 points and conceded only 60. But that was only the beginning. Starting with the visit to Widnes on Christmas Day, Warrington won 10 games in a row for the first time in the club's history to cement their spot in the all-important top four places. They finished the league season in style too, with six consecutive victories, sealing second place in the final table behind Wigan.

Northern Rugby League – top of the table

	P	W	D	L	F	A	Pts	Percent
Wigan	38	29	3	6	641	310	61	80.26
Warrington	36	27	1	8	472	279	55	76.38
Swinton	36	26	2	8	442	223	54	75.00
Hull	38	24	3	11	547	329	51	67.10

Third-placed Swinton were the visitors to Wilderspool in the Championship semi-final and, after a thrilling match, Warrington won 11-8 thanks to tries from stand-off Tommy Flynn and wingers Dickie Blackburn and Billy 'Fanny' Roberts - his 21st of the season - and a goal from centre Ned Catterall. All the points came during a spectacular first half that delighted and enthralled the crowd of 19,300. Ominously, though, Wigan thrashed fourth-placed Hull 34-0 in the other semi-final at Central Park.

Still, the stage was set for what should have been a magnificent Championship Final at Knowsley Road, St Helens, on Saturday 8 May. By now, however, readers will realise that nothing in the Warrington story is every straightforward. And, on Monday 3 May 1926, the only General Strike in Britain's history was declared in defence of miners' wages and hours.

A total of three million men, about a fifth of the adult male population, went on strike. The Championship Final went ahead as planned, but problems with transportation and financial worries combined to reduce the attendance to 20,000. Four days after the match, on Wednesday 12 May, the General Strike ended in a humiliating defeat for the Trades Union Congress.

It was a traumatic time as Ernie Day, who had just started to follow Warrington's fortunes and would later play for Halifax, recalled in an interview published in 2000: "I was born in 1918 and I remember the General Strike of 1926. My Uncle Bob had made me a wooden fort out of a tea chest and I treasured it a great deal. At the time we had no coal, in fact we had been without for weeks, either because of the strike or because my mam and dad just didn't have the money. The stark fact was that anything that would burn was used as fuel and things were so desperate that even our furniture was in jeopardy. I came downstairs one morning to go to school to find mam in our little kitchen putting the remains of my beloved fort under the boiler for the weekly wash. When she saw me she burst into tears and hugged me to her, telling me through her tears how sorry she was. I think I grew up a little during those few moments."

1926 Championship Final
Warrington versus Wigan at Knowsley Road, St Helens on 8 May 1926.
Attendance: 20,000.

Warrington had already lost three times to Wigan during the 1925-26 season, twice at Central Park and once at Wilderspool, so it was hardly a surprise that they were beaten in the Championship Final as well.

Yet the Wire made a valiant effort before losing 22-10 and scored tries through hooker Alf Peacock and scrum-half and captain Freddie Ryder with centre Ned Catterall kicking two goals.

Wigan replied with six tries of their own, three in each half. Welsh winger Johnny Ring led the way with a hat-trick with Welsh centre Tommy Howley crossing twice and South African winger Attie van Heerden adding the sixth. Fortunately for Warrington, full-back Jim Sullivan was not at his best with the boot and only added two conversions.

Ned Catterall actually gave Warrington the lead with a penalty goal after six minutes, but tries from Howley, Ring and van Heerden, plus one Sullivan conversion, put Wigan 11-2 ahead at half-time. Howley's second try extended their lead to 14-2 before Peacock's try, improved by Catterall, made the score 14-7 after 54 minutes. However, two more tries from Ring, one converted by Sullivan, put Wigan 22-7 ahead before Ryder scored a consolation try for Warrington in the last minute.

As the Final was played at the height of the General Strike there were no newspapers and hence no comprehensive match reports.

Warrington: A. Frowen, R. Blackburn, G. Walker, E. Catterall, W. Roberts, T. Flynn, F. Ryder, W. Cunliffe, A. Peacock, W. Harrop, T. Cunliffe, J. Tranter, F. Williams.
Wigan: J. Sullivan, J. Ring, T. Howley, T. Parker, A.J. van Heerden, G. Owens, D. Booysen, W. Hodder, J. Bennett, T. Beetham, G. van Rooyen, F. Stephens, J. Price.
Referee: R Robinson (Bradford).

Warrington used 29 players during the season, but their successes were firmly built on the efforts of 14 men – six forwards and eight backs. The six forwards all played in the final and were remarkably durable throughout the season: prop Billy Cunliffe with 40 appearances, hooker Alf Peacock with 40 appearances, prop Bill Harrop with 41 appearances, second-row forward Tommy Cunliffe with 40 appearances, second-row forward Jim Tranter with just 38 appearances and loose-forward Frank Williams who made 39 appearances.

The eight regular backs were almost as resolute. Scrum-half Freddie Ryder, for example, played in all 42 games while wingers Dickie Blackburn and Billy Roberts made 34 and 39 appearances respectively. All three played in the final as did full-back Arthur Frowen with 29 appearances, centre Ned Catterall with 41 appearances and stand-off Tommy Flynn who made 19 appearances. Welshman Flynn had a good excuse for his comparatively small contribution to the cause because he had only been signed from St Helens for £400 in December.

The season's two most serious injuries were also in the back division. Welsh centre Arthur Child had made 26 appearances when he suffered a broken thigh bone in the first half of the Challenge Cup first round victory at Hunslet. The injury ended his career and left him in hospital for four months. He needed a serious operation that left him with a shortened leg. Veteran full-back Ben Jolley, meanwhile, was carried off with damaged cartilage in the Challenge Cup third round defeat at Hull after 30 appearances. The injury ended his season and meant that he had to pass the captaincy on to scrum-half Freddie Ryder.

The season had started in style, though, when Fair Barber, the club president, officially opened an extension to the main stand before the game against Batley. A crowd of 9,000 was there to witness the occasion and cheer Warrington to a 13-2 victory.

It soon became apparent that the Warrington pack was something special and supporters turned out in force to watch them in action. The Lancashire Cup first round tie at Wigan attracted a crowd of 25,000, including 8,000 from Warrington, 6,000 of whom had travelled on four special trains. The game was a triumph for the Warrington forwards but the Wigan backs were a little bit too fast and too clever for their Wire counterparts and helped the home team to a 14-10 victory.

Ben Jolley, the Warrington full-back and captain, was exempt from any criticism, however, and produced a wonderful exhibition of goalkicking – eight successes from nine attempts – in the 43-16 victory over Hunslet. All good judges agreed that he was the best full-back to pull on a primrose and blue shirt.

The club's first 10-match winning run began at Widnes on Christmas Day and soon gathered momentum as Rochdale Hornets (twice), Wigan Highfield, Dewsbury and Leigh were defeated. St Helens were the seventh team to be vanquished – on a day when the club flag flew at half mast as a mark of respect for Tommy Barnes, one of the stars from the club's rugby union days, who had died at the age of 60. Barnes, a centre, was a tricky runner, a deadly tackler and an expert at kicking drop goals. His finest hour had come at Fairfield, Liverpool, in 1886 in the final of the South West Lancashire and Border Towns Cup when he sealed victory with a wonderful drop-goal.

An extension to the main stand was completed in time for the start of the 1925-26 season.

The St Helens game also marked the debut in a Warrington shirt of Reginald Gautrey, aged 22, a new signing from Northampton rugby union club. Gautrey, from Long Buckby, near Rugby, was 5 feet 10 inches tall, weighed 11 stones 9 pounds and had played for the East Midlands county team. He was regarded as the best centre in the Midlands. Later in the month, Warrington signed another rugby union centre, Ron Jones, aged 19, from Yorkley, a prominent club in the Forest of Dean. He was 5 feet 9 inches and weighed in at 12 stones. Sadly, neither player quite made the grade, but at least the club was trying to rectify the team's deficiencies.

Victories at Wigan Highfield and Barrow and at home to Leigh made it 10 wins in a row and the record-breaking run was stretched to 11 with the Challenge Cup first-round victory at Hunslet. The Hunslet match was captured on film by a Warrington supporter and became one of the highlights of the *History of the Wire* video released in 1992. The grainy, black-and-white footage showed players and officials boarding the train at Arpley Station in Warrington. Jim Tranter enjoyed a pre-match cigarette while Tom Cunliffe performed a card trick and 'Mr Warrington', Bob Anderton, kept a genial eye on proceedings. The Hunslet crowd was a mass of flat caps and bowler hats and winger Billy Roberts was seen racing in for Warrington's only try.

Batley ended the record-breaking run with an 18-10 win at Mount Pleasant, but it hardly mattered. Warrington were at home to St Helens Recs the next Saturday for a Challenge Cup second round tie that generated enormous interest – a crowd of 21,630 and record receipts for a cup tie of £1,260. Warrington returned to winning ways in style with a 17-12 victory built on tries from Billy Cunliffe, Billy Roberts and Frank Williams and four goals from Ben Jolley.

It was also seven-year-old Ernie Day's first match: "It was winter-time and there was straw piled up round the perimeter of the field," he recalled years later. "My dad took me. There was a wooden fence all the way round the ground in those days, before the wall was built. There was a chap sat on the hay who only had one leg. He was a casualty of the First World War and he knew my father. The match started and I couldn't see so my dad lifted me over the fence and sat me on the straw. I said 'It's all wet dad, my bottom's wet', so this chap said 'hang on a minute' and he put his wooden leg out and I sat on that. So I watched my first game at Wilderspool sat on a wooden leg."

Warrington were drawn away to Hull in the third round - the quarter-finals - and visited Nantwich Brine Baths in the build-up to help them relax. The ploy did not work, however, as Warrington were well beaten 15-2. The backs did not play with any confidence and the knee injury to Jolley sealed their fate in front of 20,818 fans at the Boulevard.

Worse was to follow when, at the end of March, Warrington suffered their first - and only - home defeat of the season, against Wigan. Warrington were humiliated 38-4 with Jim Sullivan kicking seven goals. It was a black Saturday for the Wire who were outpaced and outclassed. Captain Alex Reid, the local MP, was at Wilderspool to witness the slaughter.

Once again, though, Warrington bounced back with seven straight victories, six in the league and one in the Championship semi-final, before meeting their old nemesis Wigan in the final. One of the victories came against St Helens Recs in the league at Wilderspool in a game that doubled as a benefit match for Ben Jolley and Jim Fearnley and attracted a crowd of 12,000.

Each player later received a cheque for £365 from the gate receipts and other fundraising activities. The referee had to stop play for a few minutes after a quantity of the straw on the sidelines caught fire. Police, officials and some supporters worked together to extinguish the flames.

Happy days for the Wire indeed and even the club treasurer could afford to smile: Warrington's gate receipts for the season had exceeded £10,000 for the first time and the club had made a profit of £400.

There was, however, sad news in June 1926 with the death, aged 70, of William Wallington, one of the seven young men who had formed the club 50 years before at a meeting at St Paul's Church Sunday School on Bewsey Road. Wallington had been the club's first captain in the days when they were known as Warrington Zingari, based at the Patten Arms and playing their home matches at Arpley. The seven young men, known as the Founding Fathers, were Wallington, his brother Thomas Wallington, G.J. Browne, G.W. Edwards, Earnest Early, Ebenezer England and Thomas Rathbone.

Top: Warrington's team for the 1926 Championship Final at Knowsley Road. Left to right, back: Jim 'Shint' Daintith (trainer), Frank Williams, Bill Harrop, Ben Jolley, Alf Peacock, Billy Cunliffe, Tommy Cunliffe, Len Green (trainer); front: Billy Roberts, Tommy Flynn, Arthur Frowen, Jim Tranter, Dickie Blackburn, Ned Catterall, George Walker, Freddie Ryder.

Left: Welshman Tommy Flynn, pictured in St Helens kit, cost just £400 when he was signed from the Knowsley Road club in December 1925.

8. 1926-27: A new flag unfurled

Club president: Austin Crowe. Club captain: Freddie Ryder.

Sports fans in Warrington had other local heroes to admire apart from the boys in primrose and blue. Two, in particular, stood head and shoulders above the rest: jockey Steve Donoghue and cricketer George Duckworth. Both were born in Warrington and achieved international fame in their sports. Both were in the main stand at Wilderspool on Saturday 18 December 1926 to see Warrington play Wigan.

Warrington had not beaten their arch rivals for two years but, perhaps inspired by the presence of Donoghue and Duckworth, made a spectacular return to form to win a thrilling match 14-8 in front of 8,000 delighted spectators. It was an afternoon to remember, and particularly for Welsh centre Billy Rhodes, making his Wire debut after signing from the Pontypridd rugby league team. Rhodes did not get on the scoresheet himself, but his presence galvanised the Warrington threequarters and led to two tries for loose-forward Jim Tranter, one for Rhodes's fellow centre Jack Green and one for stand-off Tommy Flynn, who also kicked a goal. Rhodes went on to play 80 first-team games, scoring 31 tries and kicking 73 goals, and played for Monmouthshire in the newly-expanded County Championship. Sadly, the win over Wigan was one of the few highlights in a disappointing season.

In the summer, Warrington had continued to invest in the facilities at Wilderspool and replaced the wooden railings around the ground with a concrete wall, at a cost of £544/10/0. Another 250 seats were also added to the main stand. Yet, crucially, there were no new signings and Warrington's limitations were cruelly exposed on the opening day of the season when they were crushed 52-12 - 12 tries to two - by Wigan at Central Park. Warrington never gave up and did not play badly. They were simply crushed by the better team.

The second home game of the season, against Dewsbury, provided another shock. Before kick-off, a new flag, presented to the club by ardent supporter Sydney Davies from Lymm, was unfurled amid great cheering. Warrington also had a mystery rugby union winger from the Midlands on the right wing under the pseudonym J. Morris and he scored a try. Yet Warrington still lost 25-15 and their miserable afternoon was summed up when Bill Stockley, the former Wire winger, scored one of Dewsbury's five tries by simply stealing the ball from Ben Jolley. The full-back, sadly, was now just a shadow of his former self and never played for the first team again.

New signings were needed, although the mysterious J. Morris was not the answer and he returned home. Instead, Warrington signed Jack Parry, the Tyldesley and Lancashire rugby union winger after he had impressed in an 'A' team trial game while playing under the pseudonym J. Berry. Parry, who was 21, was 5 feet 10 inches tall and weighed 11 stones 8 pounds. All this cloak and dagger secrecy was necessary, of course, to keep the players' real identities away from the rugby union authorities who would ban any player who associated with rugby league.

More pain followed with the trip to Featherstone who built up a 27-0 lead in front of just 2,000 supporters before Welshman Tommy Flynn broke clear to score a try, one of 22 he scored in 38 appearances during the season. Flynn was easily Warrington's best player and was showing the form that had inspired one St Helens supporter to write *An Ode to Tommy Flynn*:

Here's a health to ye, Now Tommy Flynn.
Faster, and faster, and faster agin.
Powerfullest pacer, wid steps like a racer,
The other team's lacer, is our Tommy Flynn.

During the season, New Zealand were also making their second tour of Britain and there were hopes that the Kiwis' visit to Wilderspool on Saturday 9 October would attract a record crowd. The Kiwis, who were amateurs and only receiving expenses for their efforts, were based in Harrogate and arrived at Bank Quay Station at 12.45pm. They were immediately taken to Carters Café for lunch with Sir Gilbert Greenall, of the famous brewing family, and the Mayor of Warrington, Alderman Arthur Bennett.

Admission for the match was 1/6 and supporters were advised to arrive early. On the day, however, torrential rain reduced the attendance to 7,500 and Warrington won comfortably, 17-5. The Warrington forwards were dominant, allowing half-backs Freddie Ryder and Tommy Flynn to shine. Flynn crossed for two tries and Jack Parry scored his first for the club while Jim Tranter and Jack Green also got on the scoresheet. Ned Catterall kicked Warrington's only goal.

Three weeks later, Warrington suffered more injury problems when Freddie Ryder fractured a finger early in the second half at home to Oldham. Warrington were only trailing 5-4 when Ryder left the field but went on to lose 22-4. The trip to Swinton the following week did not go according to plan either. Forward Charlie Arrowsmith missed the train and his place in the team had to be taken at the last minute by veteran Tommy Cunliffe. Warrington lost 38-12.

Warrington's supporters were getting frustrated and that frustration bubbled over during the home game against Wigan Highfield. Stand-off Tommy Flynn had a try controversially disallowed by Widnes referee W. Marshall after 15 minutes for an alleged knock-on. The poor official was then barracked for the rest of the match, much to the horror of the veteran reporter from the *Warrington Guardian*.

Warrington won that match 10-5, but lost heavily at St Helens the following Saturday. Next up were Wigan at Wilderspool. The previous six meetings between the two clubs had all ended in Wigan victories: 44-4, 14-10, 20-5, 38-4, 22-10 and 52-12. This time it would be different and Donoghue and Duckworth were not the only sporting celebrities there to see the action. They brought with

Warrington with the Lancaster Charity Cup. Left to right, standing: Len Green (trainer), Jim 'Shint' Daintith (trainer), Jim Worsley, Bill Harrop, Jim Tranter, Frank Mason, Alf Peacock. Seated: Dickie Blackburn, Jack Close, Billy Rhodes, Tommy Flynn, Ron Jones, Billy Cunliffe, unknown, Jack Parry, Frank Williams, Freddie Ryder. Front: Jim Dickenson (left) and Arthur Frowen.

them two friends, Harry Makepeace and Frank Watson. Makepeace had played football and cricket for England, while with Everton and Lancashire. Watson was the Lancashire cricket all-rounder. All four enjoyed a thrilling Warrington victory.

Widnes visited Wilderspool on Christmas Day, although not every Warrington supporter was in a festive and forgiving mood. Warrington trailed by nine points after an hour but fought back to win 16-12. The victory, however, was marred by crowd trouble. Some spectators showed their disapproval of several decisions by referee Harding, of Broughton, especially when he awarded the visitors' first try. In the second half bricks were thrown onto the pitch. The referee immediately stopped play and, with Freddie Ryder, the Warrington captain, went to the touchline and appealed for calm. There was no further trouble.

January saw the usual wheeling and dealing ahead of the Challenge Cup transfer deadline. Warrington swapped centre Ned Catterall, who had been put on the transfer list, for Bill Vowles, the Bradford Northern winger. Vowles had played for Yorkshire and was described as 'dashing, forceful and speedy' but only made seven appearances, scoring one try.

Warrington also signed a young New Zealand-born loose-forward, Charlie Seeling, from the Ince All Blacks, a Wigan junior side. Seeling, who received a £100 signing-on fee, was the son of the famous All Black rugby union forward Charlie 'Bronco' Seeling, who had played for Wigan RLFC from 1909 to 1920. Seeling junior would develop into one of Warrington's greatest loose-forwards, scoring 41 tries in 195 appearances.

One of Warrington's fixtures this season was at Pontypridd. The players left Bank Quay Station at noon on the Friday and stayed overnight at the Grand

Hotel in Cardiff before moving on to Pontypridd. Five intrepid supporters made the journey by car, leaving Warrington at 6.30am on the morning of the match. They arrived safely and on time and made themselves heard with shouts of "Go on the Wire" from the main stand.

In the committee room beforehand, committee men, officials and the five Warrington supporters were delighted to meet two former Wire stalwarts from before the First World War – forward Frank Shugars and half-back Jack Jenkins. However, on hearing that Shugars, Warrington's first tourist, had fallen on hard times an impromptu collection was held to raise money for him.

Warrington were less charitable when they heard that centre Reg Gautrey, a major signing from Northampton RUFC the year before, had returned home to Long Buckby and signed professional forms to play football for Northampton Town FC. Warrington complained to the Football Association, via the Rugby League Council, and the FA immediately cancelled his registration.

The Wire's results remained patchy but supporters who watched the 'A' team saw a promising debut by an 18-year-old full-back from Cumberland, given the pseudonym F. Kimberley, when Wigan Highfield 'A' visited Wilderspool in March. He had a safe pair of hands and could kick with both feet. He played again for the 'A' team against Broughton Rangers 'A' two weeks later and again impressed. He was one for the future.

Another young player, prop-forward Jack Miller, had made his first-team debut at St Helens in December and was starting to make a name for himself until he fractured a forearm using a starting handle on a car. He missed the rest of the season. It could only happen to Warrington.

The club were rewarded for their forward thinking off the pitch. Committee member Edmund Osborne was elected chairman of the Rugby League Council, a very influential position. Also, Warrington were asked to stage two major finals, the Lancashire Cup between St Helens and St Helens Recs and the Championship between Swinton and St Helens Recs. The Lancashire Cup Final attracted a crowd of 20,720. The Championship Final was even more popular with 24,432 present. After that match, the rugby league journalist Ernest Blackwell, using the pseudonym 'Observer' in the *Daily Dispatch*, reported that: "Warrington has clearly established itself as a suitable venue for such games."

However, Warrington had been completely out of contention for honours, losing in the first round of the Lancashire Cup and the Challenge Cup and only finishing 16th in the table with more defeats, 19, than victories, 18.

But the season ended with a trophy, of sorts. Rochdale Hornets were beaten 31-18 at Lancaster on 7 May to win the Lancashire Charity Cup. Stand-off Tommy Flynn, with two tries, and centre Ron Jones, with a try and five goals, took the leading roles. The match raised more than £100 for the Lancaster Invalid Children's Aid Association. Warrington received a handsome silver cup to keep for 12 months and 'gold' medals. Perhaps next year would be better.

9. 1927-28: Drama and controversy

Club president: Austin Crowe. Club captain: Tommy Flynn.

In July 1927, the Warrington committee showed they meant business by appointing the legendary former Wire winger Jack Fish as the first-team coach and trainer. Fish was still idolised by older supporters who could remember his thrilling wing play, his exceptional speed off the mark, uncanny ability to take awkward passes and knack of stopping dead in his tracks, sending opponents whizzing into touch.

Fish had scored 215 tries in 321 appearances for Warrington between 1898 and 1911 and played in four Challenge Cup Finals. He had also kicked 262 goals and played for Lancashire and England. Fish was to be assisted by trainers Len Green and Jim 'Shint' Daintith.

Two former players, Bill Harmer and George Dickenson, were put in charge of the 'A' team. Harmer was a forward who had made 187 appearances for the first team between 1902 and 1915, scoring 15 tries and kicking two goals. Dickenson had been one of the 'Aristocratic Four' – the sensational threequarter line of Fish, Isherwood, Dickenson and Harris. He had made 375 appearances from 1900 to 1914, scoring 94 tries and also playing in four Challenge Cup Finals. During the war, Harmer had served with the Lancashire Fusiliers while Dickenson had been with the Royal Garrison Artillery. Keeping discipline was not going to be a problem.

The Warrington committee backed Fish to the hilt by making seven significant signings over the next few months. To get the ball rolling, two youngsters were signed from the New Springs amateur rugby league club in Wigan in August – winger Tommy Thompson and scrum-half Billy Kirk. Welsh forward Ponty Davies was the next to arrive, in September. Aged 22, Davies was a bustling, fast-moving runner who had played for Pontypridd RUFC before switching codes and joining Pontypridd RLFC. He had also played rugby league for Wales.

Welsh centre Jesse Meredith, aged 21, was the next to sign, at the end of September, from Abertillery RUFC and he received a £320 signing-on fee. Warrington officials travelled to South Wales to watch Newport play Abertillery and signed him after the match. Meredith was a strong tackler and weighed in at 12 stones 7 pounds. He was also a total oddball who pretended to his new team-mates that he could speak fluent Welsh by uttering phrases which were, in fact, complete gibberish. He also hated to be called by his Christian name Jesse, preferring to be addressed by his nickname 'Kikey'.

Another Welsh centre, Les Perkins, followed one week later from Cross Keys RUFC in South Wales with Warrington agreeing to pay out £475 as a signing-on fee. The 22-year-old had twice been a reserve for Wales the previous season, including for their match at Twickenham. Perkins, whose slightly bowed legs would make him a great favourite with newspaper cartoonists, made his debut in a 12-12 draw with Salford at Wilderspool, but then broke an ankle in training and was ruled out until January.

In many ways, the next signing was the boldest of the lot with Warrington paying Broughton Rangers a then club record £650 for Dai Davies at the end of November. He had been on their transfer list at £850 but appealed to the Rugby League Council about the size of the fee. The negotiations between Warrington and Broughton took a week to complete but, once they were, Warrington finally had a suitable replacement for the injured Freddie Ryder.

Davies, who was 5 feet 7 inches tall and weighed 10 stones, may have lacked tact but there were two things he was not short of – ability and confidence. He even made sure that he received a £250 signing-on fee by letting the committee know that he would be meeting officials from Oldham the following day unless they paid up.

And, unlike Meredith, he could speak Welsh. In fact it was his first language and Meredith's bizarre ramblings were quickly exposed for what they were. Despite this, however, the pair became great friends.

Davies was a success from the very start, with his pace and quick, accurate passing to Tommy Flynn adding a new dimension to Warrington's play. His home debut came against Dewsbury, in a match that produced a thrilling finale. Dewsbury, the Yorkshire Cup holders, led 15-13 with four minutes left. Warrington were attacking constantly but could find no way through until Billy Rhodes played the ball, collected it himself and forced his way over near the posts. The home supporters went wild and hats and walking sticks were thrown into the air. Flynn kicked the goal to seal an 18-15 victory.

The seventh major signing, that of the 19-year-old Cumbrian full-back Billy Holding in January, was very much one for the future. Holding, from Maryport, had played some trial games for the 'A' team - it was he who appeared under the name of Kimberley the previous season - and impressed all concerned with his goalkicking.

Most of the new players had arrived too late to have much influence on Warrington's league campaign – they finished 17th in the table – but were bedding in nicely by the start of the Challenge Cup.

Warrington were drawn away to Kinsley, a mining village near Pontefract, in the first round, but the amateurs accepted £150 to play the tie at Wilderspool. Warrington selected an all-Welsh threequarter line – Rhodes, Meredith, Perkins, Flynn – and between them they scored seven of Warrington's 11 tries in a 43-2 victory. Rhodes scored four of the tries.

Victories away to Hull Kingston Rovers and at home to Huddersfield followed, before Warrington were paired with high-flying Leeds in the semi-final at Rochdale. Ten days before the big match, however, tragedy befell their goalkicking winger Billy Rhodes. His seven-year-old brother Cyril, who had been visiting his house, ran out in front of a lorry on Bank Quay Bridge and was killed instantly. An inquest jury returned a verdict of 'death by misadventure' with the coroner recording that the boy had been living in the wilds of Wales and was not used to heavy road traffic.

Rhodes missed the next league match, at home to Hull KR, but bravely returned for the semi-final when a crowd of 22,000 assembled at the Athletic Ground to see Warrington win 9-2. The only try came in the second half when Billy Kirk capitalised on a mistake by Jim Brough, the Leeds full-back and captain, and snapped up the loose ball, raced clear and went over behind the posts. Rhodes kicked the goal and two penalty goals to send Warrington through to the Final.

Four days before the Final, the last before the move to Wembley in 1929, Warrington had to fulfil a league fixture at Hunslet and, not surprisingly, sent a side full of youngsters. The Parksiders ran riot, inflicting a 68-14 loss, a club record that would stand for 68 years. Warrington were losing 35-0 at half-time, conceded 16 tries in all and, to cap a miserable afternoon, prop Jack Miller was sent off, along with a Hunslet player, for fighting. Warrington were later fined £15 for fielding a weakened team. That defeat, and the defeat in the Final, formed part of a losing streak that stretched to eight games, a club record that would last for 69 years.

1928 Challenge Cup Final
Warrington versus Swinton at Central Park, Wigan, on 14 April 1928.
Attendance: 33,909.

The final provided drama and controversy. The drama involved the 'death' of a player, the controversy cost Warrington the cup.

Warrington scrum-half Billy Kirk, who was concussed early in the second half, was the unfortunate player. The game was held up for five minutes while he was treated and eventually he was placed on a stretcher and carried off the pitch.

Two men walking alongside the stretcher happened to be wearing shirts with collars - a rumour started among the spectators that they were priests and that Kirk had been read his last rites and died. Even team-mate Dai Davies was caught up in the confusion.

"I will never forget it," wrote Davies in his autobiography *Man of Amman: The Life of Dai Davies*. "Billy was flat out and there was steam coming from him. He'd had a rabbit punch or something and he was steaming. There was a lot of fuss. Billy was a Catholic and so they brought the priest on. They thought he was dead. Then they carried him off."

Thankfully, the rumours were not true, although Kirk was out of action for the rest of the season. Warrington, who were trailing 3-0 at the time following a try from Swinton winger Chris Brockbank, switched Davies from the wing to his preferred scrum-half position and moved Charlie Seeling from loose-forward to the wing.

Substitutes were not allowed at this time, of course, and so Warrington had to play for the rest of the match with 12 men. Incredibly, Seeling scored a try in the corner to level the scores at 3-3 and fuel hopes of a remarkable victory. Sadly, it was not to be, although the manner of their 5-3 defeat would remain a source of bitterness for years to come.

Brockbank, who would later become the Warrington club secretary, hoisted a huge kick up field towards Arthur Frowen, the Warrington full-back, who had been kicking and tackling immaculately and had been their best player.

Billy Kirk

The wind carried the ball over Frowen's head and he touched it down behind his own try line. The referee, however, ruled that Frowen had first touched the ball in the field of play and awarded a five-yard scrum, with Swinton's head and feed, instead of a 25-yard drop out. Swinton duly won possession and fed the ball back to centre Jack Evans who kicked a drop goal to win the cup. It was a heart-breaking way for the 12 men of Warrington to be denied.

Warrington: A. Frowen, W.H. Rhodes, J.O. Meredith, L.J. Perkins, D.M. Davies, T. Flynn, W. Kirk, W. Cunliffe, A. Peacock, J. Miller, J. Tranter, F. Williams, C. Seeling jnr.
Swinton: W. Young; F. Evans, H. Halsall, J. Evans, C. Brockbank; A. Atkinson, B. Rees, M.F. Strong, H. Blewer, H.E. Morris, M. Hodgson, R.H. Cracknell, F. Beswick.
Referee: H. Horsfall (Batley).

At least Warrington finished the season on a high note with a 30-20 victory at Dewsbury, with Billy Rhodes scoring two tries to take his tally for the season to 22. Even the committee men had expected Warrington to lose and had only taken losing money with them. The players had to wait until the following Monday morning to collect their winning pay from Wilderspool.

Dai Davies, Ponty Davies, Jack Miller, Frank Williams and Tommy Flynn all played in trials for that summer's Great Britain tour to Australia and New Zealand, although none were selected. Committee man Edmund Osborne was, however, appointed joint manager for the trip, as he had been four years earlier.

Not surprisingly, after such an outlay on new players, Warrington's accounts showed a loss of £943/10/8d on the season. The Supporters' Club had done their bit, however, by paying for the scoreboard and clock at the Fletcher Street end of the ground which would become a familiar landmark until it was condemned by safety officers and demolished in 1989.

The Cunliffe brothers, Billy and Tommy, were approaching the end of their glorious careers and were rewarded with a joint benefit which raised £187/17/8d for each player. Yet Billy, in particular, was still a force to be reckoned with and was the only Warrington player in the Lancashire team who thrashed Yorkshire

35-19 in the County Championship match at Wilderspool on 29 October in front of 12,000 fans.

Warrington were still one of the forward-thinking clubs and, at the Rugby Football League's annual meeting, they proposed a two-division scheme, but their plan was defeated. Warrington were also embroiled in some controversy when a player called Matthew Roston signed for both them and Wigan Highfield. The RFL suspended him until 31 October and ruled that he would be a Warrington player after that, having signed for them first.

Among the past players who died during the season was Tommy Knight, who had joined Warrington from Latchford Rangers as a full-back and made 44 appearances from 1901 to 1907. Upon retiring as a professional player, he had joined the Walker's Brewery amateur team.

A local hero: George Duckworth

George Duckworth was one of the finest wicketkeepers of his generation whose devotion to the Wire was such that, in his later years, he became a director of the club.

Duckworth was born at 17 Selby Street, Warrington, on 9 May 1907 and made his name as a young cricketer with the Warrington club before joining Lancashire in 1922. He was small in stature but big in heart and voice.

He made his first-class debut the following summer and would go on to make more than 500 appearances for his native county before his retirement in 1938. More significantly, he was a key member of five County Championship-winning teams. In 1929 he was one of the *Wisden* Cricketers of the Year after enjoying a memorable summer in 1928 when he dismissed 107 batsmen: 77 caught and 30 stumped. Duckworth, who was famous for the piercing volume of his "Owzat" appeals, also played test cricket for England from 1924 to 1936, appearing in 24 tests and touring Australia.

Throughout it all, he was an avid Warrington rugby league fan and, in 1953, he provided the commentary for the first hospital radio broadcast from Wilderspool when Warrington beat Workington Town 10-2 in the second round of the Challenge Cup. Workington were the Challenge Cup holders at the time.

In 1961, he became a Warrington director and he maintained his interest in the club until the end of his life. On New Year's Day 1966, four days before he died, he watched Warrington 'A' beat Wigan 'A' 40-5 at Wilderspool in the morning before travelling to Wigan in the afternoon to see the two first teams play.

Guerrilla warfare: Gitts, the cartoonist with the Manchester-based *Daily Dispatch* newspaper, saw the 1928 Challenge Cup final as little more than a wrestling match.

10. 1928-29: The try of a lifetime

Club president: Austin Crowe. Club captain: Billy Cunliffe.

Jack Fish started to suffer health problems during the summer of 1928 and so the Warrington committee had to find a new trainer. The man they turned to was Jim Heesom, who was well known locally for training athletes, and he proved to be a sound appointment. "What he does not know about getting a man fit is not worth knowing, and he looks like making a worthy successor to Jack Fish," wrote Bob Anderton in the programme for the opening home game.

The committee also made another inspired signing when, on Thursday 6 September, they paid Broughton Rangers £600 for their 22-year-old centre Billy Dingsdale. The player himself received £100, paid in four instalments. To put the signing into perspective, the world record fee at the time was only £1,000.

Dingsdale, who was 5 feet 11 inches tall and weighed just over 12 stones, was a wonderfully creative centre and made his debut, alongside his brother, Ben, who was already on Warrington's books, for the 'A' team against Broughton 'A' at Wilderspool. A crowd of 4,000 turned up and were rewarded with a Billy Dingsdale try in a 22-6 victory. At the same time the first team were losing 10-0 at Broughton, in front of just 3,000 fans, in a match that contained 77 scrums – almost one a minute.

Billy Dingsdale's first team debut came the following Saturday against Hunslet at Wilderspool. The match, incidentally, kicked off at 3.20pm rather than 3.30pm to allow the Hunslet players to catch an earlier train back to Yorkshire. Inevitably, Dingsdale scored a try in a 41-2 victory and tries followed at regular intervals throughout the season as he became the leading try scorer with 28 in 33 matches, equalling the club record set by Jack Fish in 1909-10.

When Dingsdale was signed it was hoped that he would be able link up again with scrum-half Dai Davies, his former team-mate at Broughton Rangers. Davies, however, had suffered a knee cartilage injury in training and would only play four games all season, which allowed his stand-in Billy Kirk an extended run in the team.

"Surely no club could have worse luck than Warrington," Bob Anderton lamented in the programme for the Hunslet game. "After training most assiduously during the summer months and playing brilliantly in the opening two games, Dai has had the shocking luck to develop a loose cartilage, and he will not be available to play for some months. As a matter of fact, he was admitted to a nursing home in Manchester last Thursday, and he is to be operated upon this afternoon by Mr Douglas, the gentleman who has been so successful with our previous injured players – and goodness knows we have had above our share! It is most unfortunate coming at a time when we seem to have got together a most useful side, and especially as Dai lately remarked he never felt so fit in his life. Well, we are lucky to possess a most capable substitute, and officials, players, members and supporters wish this most enthusiastic and whole-hearted player a speedy and complete recovery."

Dingsdale did, however, strike up an impressive left-wing pairing with Tommy 'Tubby' Thompson. Tubby was not built for speed, but if he was given the ball 20 yards out with just one man to beat a try was almost guaranteed because he had a wonderful sidestep.

Dingsdale had the ability to do just that and he was an expert at a skill not seen today: approaching an opponent at top speed, chipping the ball over his head with the outside of his boot, accelerating round the player and catching the ball before it landed. Dingsdale also played in every representative game for which he was eligible, two for England, scoring three tries, and three for Lancashire, helping them to win the County Championship.

Against Oldham at Wilderspool in January, he also scored what was described as the "try of a lifetime". Early in the second half he took a pass from Tommy Flynn in his own half and then seemed to beat the entire Oldham team before touching down. His effort earned him a standing ovation and comparisons with the great Jack Fish.

Warrington made another major signing in November when they paid Wigan Highfield £400 for their goalkicking winger Tommy Blinkhorn. Highfield had financial problems and Warrington completed the deal after a 2-2 draw at the club. It is safe to assume that Blinkhorn, aged 23, was a good tackler because when his rugby league career was over he became a professional wrestler. Like Dingsdale, he made an impressive debut with two tries and five goals in a 31-0 victory over Featherstone Rovers at Wilderspool on 1 December, a day that prop-forward Jack Miller would never forget. He got married at Winwick Church in the morning and played for Warrington in the afternoon.

Victories over both St Helens clubs, St Helens Recs in the first round and St Helens in the second round, had raised hopes of success in the Lancashire Cup. Warrington were drawn away to Widnes in the semi-final for a game that attracted a crowd of 14,000, including jockey Steve Donoghue. Warrington, however, were outplayed and lost 25-5 with Billy Dingsdale and Billy Rhodes the only backs to escape criticism in a comprehensive defeat.

Wilderspool was then chosen to stage the Final between Wigan and Widnes and a crowd of 19,000 saw the men from Central Park win 5-4. Warrington's own form, however, remained inconsistent until Christmas Day when they avenged the semi-final defeat by beating Widnes 19-5 with winger Tommy Blinkhorn scoring a hat-trick of tries. Another famous winger, Jack Fish, was still in the club's thoughts. He was not in the best of health and a ground collection on the day raised £26 to help him out. That would be worth £2,600 today.

The win over Widnes was the start an amazing run of 11 consecutive victories, including a league double over Bradford Northern who were struggling

Warrington were presented with a new kit in September 1928, one which included, for the first time, the borough coat of arms badge. Left to right, back: Jack Miller, Charlie Seeling (jnr), Jesse Meredith, Jim Tranter, Frank Williams, Alf Peacock, Arthur Frowen, Billy Dingsdale; front: Tommy Flynn, Les Perkins, Billy Cunliffe, Billy Roberts, Billy Rhodes, Billy Kirk.

at the foot of the table. Warrington won 35-7 at Bradford in front of just 600 fans with Billy Dingsdale crossing for four of the nine tries and kicking a goal. Two weeks later, Dingsdale again scored four tries as Northern were thrashed 65-0 at Wilderspool. This time, however, Tommy Blinkhorn took the individual scoring honours by kicking nine goals to equal the club record set by Jack Fish in 1906 and equalled by George Thomas in 1909. He also scored two tries for a match haul of 24 points.

After losing the 1928 Challenge Cup Final in controversial circumstances, Warrington were determined to go one better in 1929 and, for once, enjoyed the luck of the draw with three consecutive home ties. Leeds were the visitors in the first round, attracting 22,587 fans, including 5,000 of their own supporters. Warrington went in front after just three minutes when loose-forward Charlie Seeling picked the ball up from the base of a scrum and passed to stand-off Tommy Flynn who scored under the crossbar. Tommy Blinkhorn kicked the goal and added a clinching try in the second half for an 8-0 victory. It was the first time Leeds had failed to score that season.

Oldham were the visitors in round 2 and another huge crowd, 22,947, packed into Wilderspool to see Warrington record their 11th successive victory, 7-0. Second-row forward Frank Williams, who scored Warrington's only try, and scrum-half Billy Kirk were outstanding, while winger Tommy Blinkhorn, despite being injured in the early stages, converted the try and kicked a penalty goal.

Warrington were paired with Dewsbury in the third round with the first Wembley Final now just two matches away. Another large crowd, this time 21,201, rolled up. Before the kick-off, some of the straw that had been used to protect the pitch from frost – and was still on the sidelines – caught fire. The flames were quickly extinguished and there were no fireworks on the pitch, either, not for Warrington anyway, who lost 10-4.

Dewsbury went on to reach the Final, where they lost 13-2 to Wigan, and Lord Daresbury, one of Warrington's vice-presidents, presented the cup and the medals. As it was the first Wembley Final, Warrington organised a special dining train for 500 supporters to see history being made. A tradition that continues until this day had begun.

Warrington finished seventh in the league, a massive improvement on the 17th place of the previous campaign, and that was reflected in increased attendances and programme sales. The programme, for example, made a profit of £89/13/2, up 50 per cent on the previous season.

Warrington's 'A' team also performed well. They finished top of their table and then beat Swinton 5-0 in the 'A' team Championship final at Wigan. As ever, there was hope for the future.

On a point of fashion, Warrington wore a new design of jerseys for the first time against Broughton Rangers at Wilderspool on 29 September 1928. They were white with a broad primrose and blue band around the middle and a silk borough coat of arms badge on the chest. The jerseys were paid for by Sydney Davies of Lymm, a Warrington vice-president who had presented the club with a primrose and blue flag two years earlier. The jerseys were only to be worn on special occasions.

Away from sport, at the general election on 30 May 1929, Charles Dukes regained the Warrington seat for the Labour Party, beating the Conservative candidate, Noel Goldie KC, into second place. The Liberal candidate, Miss Alison Garland, lost her deposit.

The seat changed hands again - it was becoming a key marginal - in October 1931 when Goldie defeated Dukes by 5,345 votes in a two-horse race. The turnout was almost 90 per cent. The Conservatives retained the seat, albeit with a much reduced majority, in the election of November 1935.

After his defeat in 1931, Dukes never contested the seat again but remained a major figure in Labour politics. He was general secretary of the National Union of General and Municipal Workers between 1934 and 1946 and was made a CBE in 1942. He was president of the Trades Union Congress in 1946 and a director of the Bank of England in 1947. Finally, on 1 April 1947, to the horror of some of his more ideological former Labour supporters, he was created the first, and last, Baron Dukeston of Warrington. He died the following year.

A Wilderspool hero: Billy Dingsdale

Billy Dingsdale was described as "the doyen of Lancashire centres" and it is easy to understand why. From his debut in September 1928 to his final appearance in May 1940, Dingsdale scored 154 tries for Warrington and that only tells half of the story.

His pace and eye for an opening also created dozens of tries for his wingers, most notably Tommy 'Tubby' Thompson with whom he struck up an almost telepathic understanding. Quality on that scale, of course, costs money and Warrington had to pay Broughton Rangers £600 for his services.

Dingsdale, then aged 23, had been in dispute with Broughton and was not playing for them. So when he made his debut for Warrington's 'A' team alongside his brother Ben, who was already at Wilderspool, it was to recapture some match fitness.

Inevitably, he scored a try and was promoted to the first team the following week. Dingsdale scored 28 tries in 33 appearances that first season, 1928-29, to equal the then club record set by the legendary winger Jackie Fish. The tries, and the outstanding performances, kept on coming, making him a favourite with the fans, the headline writers and the rugby league selectors.

While at Wilderspool, he played 14 times for Lancashire, seven times for England and three times for Great Britain. He also went on the 1932 tour of Australia and New Zealand.

With Warrington he collected two Lancashire Cup winners' medals, in 1929 and 1932, but also fell foul of the 'So close to Glory' curse, being a member of two Challenge Cup Final losing teams, in 1933 and 1936, and two Championship Final losing teams in 1935 and 1937.

Fittingly, though, he scored Warrington's first Wembley try, against Huddersfield in 1933, and he also scored Warrington's only try in the 1935 Championship Final against Swinton.

When he retired from playing, Dingsdale became a publican in his native St Helens and died, aged 60, in 1965. But his stylish centre play has not been forgotten at Warrington and, in January 2003, he was one of the first 12 past players to be inducted into the club's Hall of Fame.

Dingsdale's Dummy: *Daily Dispatch* cartoonist Gannon salutes Billy Dingsdale after a brilliant performance at Oldham in January 1934.

11. 1929-30: Tubby Thompson's finest hour

Club president: Austin Crowe. Club captain: Les Perkins.

After eight years without a trophy, Warrington supporters were getting restless. Salvation was at hand, however, in the shape of the Lancashire Cup, although as usual it was not going to be easy. Warrington had to play three games to reach the Final and, each time, they were drawn away from home.

The luck of the draw was particularly cruel because the club had spent a lot of money on ground improvements during the summer. An old stand had been demolished and a new one built to provide shelter for 1,500 supporters. The ground's capacity had been increased by 3,000 by providing extra terracing, using more than 250 tons of ashes. In addition, 175 tip-up seats had been bought for the main stand, with the promise that more would be purchased when finances allowed. Wilderspool was now one of the best stadiums in the game.

After all that effort, it was almost inevitable that Warrington would be drawn away in the first round of the Lancashire Cup and their visit to Leigh was played out in front of a 10,000 crowd. Warrington won a pulsating match 6-3 with prop Jack Miller, who was Leigh born-and-bred, using great strength to force his way over for their first try. Winger Tommy Blinkhorn then sealed the victory with an interception try from just inside his own half. Next up was a Thursday afternoon appointment in Barrow where tries from new captain Les Perkins, winger Tommy Blinkhorn and centre Billy Dingsdale secured a 9-7 win.

The third away day, a trip to Oldham in the semi-finals, was the toughest of the lot as the game was played in treacherous conditions, heavy ground and torrential rain. Warrington, with back-row forwards Jesse Meredith, Frank Williams and Charlie Seeling all outstanding, adapted better to the conditions and were rewarded with a 7-5 victory.

Salford were Warrington's opponents in the Final at Central Park on Saturday 23 November, but they were swept aside thanks to spectacular tries from scrum-half Billy Kirk, second-rower Jesse Meredith and winger Tommy Blinkhorn, who had scored in every round. Full-back Billy Holding, as well as having a fine game in open play, also kicked three goals to seal a 15-2 victory in front of a crowd of 21,012. The team was honoured with a civic reception on their return to Warrington followed by tea in Carter's Cafe. Large crowds lined the route to catch a glimpse of their heroes.

Prop Billy Cunliffe and hooker Alf Peacock were the only survivors of the 1921 team to collect a second winners' medal in 1929. Peacock only just made it. The match against Salford was his 367th and final appearance in primrose and blue stretching back over 10 years. His tremendous loyalty and durability had already been recognised the previous week with a benefit match against Hull at Wilderspool in front of 7,020 supporters. Peacock was given the gate receipts of £340 and a ground collection at half-time raised a further £59.

The Warrington team who beat Hunslet 30-22 at Wilderspool on 28 September 1929. Left to right, standing: Jesse Meredith, Charlie Seeling, Jack Miller, Bill Jones (reserve), Billy Cunliffe, Sam Hardman, Frank Williams, Jim Heesom (trainer). Seated: Dai Davies, Tommy Blinkhorn, Les Perkins (captain), Billy Dingsdale, Billy 'Fanny' Roberts. Kneeling: Len Green (trainer), Tommy Flynn and Billy Holding, who kicked six goals.

Four weeks after the Final, Warrington achieved an even more remarkable victory against the touring Kangaroos. Warrington had a fine record against the Australians dating back to their first tour in 1908, with two wins, a draw and just one defeat from their four visits but this time, surely, the odds were stacked against them.

The Kangaroos had already paid one visit to Wilderspool, in September, when they beat Lancashire 29-14 in front of 24,000 spectators – an impressive gate that remains Lancashire's record home crowd. There were other reasons, too, for Warrington to be worried. Loose-forward Charlie Seeling was injured while four other first-team players were on County Championship duty. Goalkicking full-back Billy Holding was representing Cumberland while first-choice half-backs Tommy Flynn and Dai Davies and back-row forward Jesse Meredith were playing for Glamorgan and Monmouthshire. Consequently, an unknown rugby union trialist with the pseudonym Taylor was drafted in to make his debut in the key role of stand-off.

Warrington were facing mission impossible but young winger Tommy 'Tubby' Thompson rose to the occasion magnificently, scoring all their points in a 17-8 win with three tries and four goals in front of 12,826 disbelieving fans. His place in the club's Hall of Fame was secure.

'Observer', writing in the Manchester-based *Daily Dispatch* newspaper, summed it up perfectly. "In the days to come when the present generation of supporters and players have given way to those coming up, and great games are recalled, folk will refer to last Saturday's match, with pride and joy. They will tell how one Thompson – a slip of a lad – scored all Warrington's 17 points against the Kangaroos captained by Tom Gorman."

'Observer' added: "The match will go down in club annals as 'Thompson's Triumph'. I am told he is not yet 21, so he has room for further development. He does not appear fast, but Saturday's match proved that he is endowed with courage and wants little room to work in. He scored all Warrington's three tries, converted two of them, and landed two penalty goals.

"Dingsdale made the opening for the first try after 10 minutes and the second was the best of the match. Kirk gave Thompson the ball near the centre. He handed off Holmes and then side-stepped McMillan to race clear and score behind the posts. For a period in the second half it looked as if the Australians might recover. Then Perkins broke through and Thompson, taking a high pass very cleverly, scored at the corner and improved with a splendid touch line effort."

Success, of course, breeds success and so, in January, Warrington were able to sign the Lancashire, England and Great Britain hooker Nat Bentham from Halifax for £400 to succeed Alf Peacock. Bentham, aged 27, was 5 feet 9 inches tall, weighed 14 stones and was a teetotaller. He had toured Australia and New Zealand with Great Britain in the summer of 1928 while with the Wigan Highfield club. His comment on signing for Warrington was straightforward: "You can rely on me doing my best whilst I am wearing a primrose and blue jersey."

Bentham played in all four tests against Australia – the first two as a Halifax player and the last two as a Warrington player – and so was one of nine Warrington players to earn representative honours during the season. Tommy Blinkhorn and Billy Dingsdale also played for Great Britain. Bentham, Dingsdale and Billy Kirk played for England; Dai Davies and Jesse Meredith played for Wales, while Blinkhorn and Davies both played for a Northern League XIII. Inevitably, because representative games were often played on the same days as league games, this took its toll on Warrington's league campaign and they only finished eighth. But as usual, the Challenge Cup set pulses racing. Warrington trailed 2-0 at half-time in their first round tie at Huddersfield before half-backs Dai Davies and Tommy Flynn created some space for Billy Dingsdale. He, in turn, fed Tommy Thompson who raced over at the corner before grounding the ball five yards in. Full-back Billy Holding landed a magnificent goal to clinch a 5-2 victory.

A dour second-round struggle against Leigh at Wilderspool followed with Warrington winning 12-3 in front of 20,000 fans. The highlight of the match was a great try by Tommy Flynn, the Warrington stand-off, who broke clear from halfway and beat man after man to score an amazing solo effort.

Warrington were drawn away to Wigan, the holders, in the quarter-finals in a tie that generated unprecedented interest. A record crowd of 39,007 packed into Central Park, beating the 35,000 who had seen the 1927 Final between Oldham and Swinton. A Billy Holding penalty goal after four minutes put Warrington ahead before Billy Dingsdale raced away and beat full-back Jim Sullivan to put Warrington into a 5-0 lead.

Wigan levelled the scores a minute before the break when winger Johnny Ring scrambled over for a try wide out that Sullivan converted on the stroke of half-time. It was a huge psychological blow to Warrington and Wigan dominated the second half with tries from loose-forward John Sherrington, Johnny Ring and centre Roy Kinnear. Sullivan improved the last try to cap a 16-5 victory.

Yet, the potency of the Warrington threequarter line in the 1929-30 season could be measured by the fact that three of its members – Tommy Blinkhorn, Billy Dingsdale and Tommy Thompson – all scored more than 20 tries. Dingsdale again led the way with 25, closely followed by Thompson with 22, while Blinkhorn touched down 21 times and was the only ever-present, playing in all 44 of Warrington's fixtures.

As well as the two games against Australia, Wilderspool also successfully staged the County Championship match between Glamorgan and Monmouthshire and Lancashire, and the Challenge Cup semi-final between Widnes and Barrow. They attracted crowds of 9,000 and 25,500 respectively to earn Wilderspool the tag of a 'sure gate venue' from the rugby league writers of the day. The investment in facilities had paid off. All that was needed now was more success on the pitch.

The 1929-30 season was also tinged with sadness following the deaths of former players William Dennett and Charlie Stowell, both aged 25. Dennett, who died in January, had been a popular member of Warrington's 'A' team. He suffered an injury to his right knee while playing for the Orford Tannery side and tetanus set in some days later. Tragically, in the days before anti-biotics were available, that infection proved fatal.

Stowell, who died in Salford Royal Hospital in May after slipping into a diabetic coma, was the captain of Broughton Rangers but had played for Warrington's 'A' team earlier in his career. He had also made one appearance for Warrington's first team, in 1925, before reviving his career with Cadishead and being snapped up by Broughton. At the Cliff he had made 89 appearances, primarily as a full-back noted for his safe pair of hands and powerful kick. He had twice been a reserve for Lancashire and would have played for England against Other Nationalities but for injury.

Pass masters: Charlie Seeling gets the ball away in front of a packed main stand. Dai Davies is the other Warrington player pictured. Both their Warrington careers ran from 1927 to 1934.

Civic reception: Captain Les Perkins shows off the Lancashire Cup to Councillor Frank Stringer, the Mayor of Warrington.

Centre Les Perkins was Warrington's captain for the 1929-30 season and led the Wire to a Lancashire Cup triumph and to victory over the touring Australians.

12. 1930-31: All roads led to Wilderspool

Club president: Austin Crowe. Club captain: Nat Bentham.

Eleven special trains were needed to take all the Warrington supporters to Leeds for the Challenge Cup semi-final against York on Saturday 28 March 1931 and the fans had every right to be optimistic. After all, Warrington had already knocked Wigan out of the Cup.

The two Lancashire rivals had been drawn against each other in the first round for a tie that captured the town's imagination. The game did not kick off until 3.30pm but, from noon onwards, all roads led to Wilderspool. A record crowd of 27,100 was eventually shoehorned inside the ground, including 8,000 from Wigan, and they paid record receipts of £1,636/4/0d. They were treated to one of the finest matches ever played on the ground, a game that neither side deserved to lose.

After 12 minutes, Warrington winger Tommy Thompson intercepted a pass and broke away with Billy Dingsdale in support. Approaching Jim Sullivan, the Wigan full-back, Thompson passed inside to his centre who cantered away for an unimproved try - first blood to Warrington.

Six minutes later, during a Wigan attack, centre Gwyn Davies dropped the ball and Dingsdale kicked ahead. He was too fast for his opponents and grabbed his second try, with Billy Holding adding the goal to make the score 8-0.

Wigan loose-forward John Sherrington then picked up and touched down under the posts for Sullivan to add the goal: 8-5. As half-time approached Warrington attacked again and the ball was kicked over the Wigan line. Frank Williams, following up, scored an easy try and Holding's second goal meant Warrington led 13-5 at the break.

Back came Wigan with Sullivan cutting the advantage with two penalty goals before Roy Kinnear scored in the corner to make the score 13-12. Sullivan's kick from the touchline just drifted wide.

Wigan winger Johnny Ring then had a try disallowed for knocking down the corner flag before touching down. The tension was becoming unbearable. Finally, 30 seconds from time, Warrington forward Bill Jones dribbled the ball over the line for an unimproved try and a 16-12 victory. Dingsdale's opportunism and splendid tackling from the rest of the backs had seen Warrington through.

St Helens Recs were the visitors to Wilderspool in the second round for another epic tie. After training on the Thursday afternoon before the match, the Warrington players were treated to tea by the committee and then went to the town's Royal Court Theatre to see the comedy *None so Blind* by Armitage Owen. It was good for team spirit. Another massive crowd, this time 24,099, including 7,000 from St Helens, packed into Wilderspool and they witnessed a tense, dour struggle that the Wire won 9-0 thanks to three goals from full-back Billy Holding and a try from Tommy Thompson.

Wembley was the word on everyone's lips, even though Warrington faced a tricky trip to Wigan Highfield in the quarter-finals for a match that was played on a bone-hard pitch in a snowstorm. Warrington built up a 12-0 lead by half-time before, at the start of the second half, Dingsdale sealed victory with a brilliant solo try. He raced away from his own line, leaving would-be tacklers in his wake, until he had just the full-back to beat. Showing tremendous composure, Dingsdale simply kicked ahead, regained possession and touched down. Warrington won 17-3.

And so the Wire headed to Headingley for the semi-final. On the Sunday before the game Nat Bentham, the Warrington captain, addressed a sportsmen's service at the Working Men's Mission in Thewlis Street: "Sport makes men of us," he told the congregation. "It makes us always strive to keep our lives clean and our bodies fit. We must always play the game. If we learn to keep our tempers and play the game on the field while young, we will grow up and play the game of life in the same way.

"Always help your committee and, whatever your own feelings, stand by your captain. The team spirit always pays and we must try to put into life what we would on the field. The Captain of life wants our co-operation and, if His example is followed, the reward is victory."

If any man deserved to lead his team out at Wembley, it was Nat Bentham. Warrington began the semi-final full of confidence and took a 5-0 lead with a try under the posts from stand-off Tommy Flynn which was converted by full-back Billy Holding, but then disaster struck. Outstanding scrum-half Dai Davies suffered a badly bruised shoulder and had to go off, leaving Warrington to play for the best part of an hour with 12 men.

Warrington reorganised – Billy Dingsdale switched to scrum-half, winger Tommy Blinkhorn moved into the centres and Bill Jones was withdrawn from the pack and put on the wing – but found themselves starved of possession. York, the underdogs, gradually took command, ground Warrington down, and went on to win 15-5 in front of a packed house of 32,419. The cup run, which had been the highlight of the season, was over.

Not surprisingly, Warrington's league campaign had suffered as the cup run had gathered momentum and they only finished 10th in the final table, one place above York. Still, there had been some notable highlights, such as winger Thompson scoring four tries in the 31-9 victory over Widnes at Wilderspool on Christmas Day. All four were described in match reports at the time as "brilliant".

Thompson finished the season with 28 tries to equal the club record that had been set by Jack Fish in 1909-10 and matched by Billy Dingsdale in 1928-29. Thompson played in all but one of Warrington's 43 matches.

However, the individual scoring honours went to Billy Holding who became the first Warrington player to kick 100 goals in a season when he kicked two in a 16-0 victory over at Leigh in the last match to take his tally to 101. He also kicked seven goals for Cumberland.

The Warrington team who beat Hull 29-4 at Wilderspool on 17 January 1931 in the league. Inset: Frank Mason. Left to right, standing: Jim Heesom (trainer), Charlie Seeling, Billy Kirk, Bill Jones, Arthur Crowe (president), Les Perkins, Len Connolly, Billy Holding, Frank Williams. Seated: Tommy Flynn, Billy Dingsdale, Jack Miller, Nat Bentham (captain), Tommy Thompson, Tommy Blinkhorn, Jim Marsden. Kneeling: Dai Davies and Len Green (trainer).

Warrington's final game at Wilderspool, a meaningless end-of-season affair against Hull Kingston Rovers, attracted just 1,500 supporters. So, at half-time, the gates were opened to allow an army of unemployed fans in for free. Economically, these were depressed and difficult days, making the committee's good housekeeping - the club made a profit of £105 on the season - all the more commendable.

The committee also announced two major signings for the following season, Australian centres Bill Shankland and Bill 'Nelson' Hardy from the Eastern Suburbs club in Sydney. Shankland, aged 25, who had been one of the stars of the 1929-30 Kangaroos tour of England, was to be paid £550 in advance with the promise of £6 per week to follow. He was 5 feet 11 inches tall and weighed 12 stones 6 pounds. Hardy, aged 22, who had also played test rugby league for Australia, agreed terms of £400 up front with £5 per week. He was 5 feet 9 inches tall and weighed 12 stones 2 pounds. "I was the highest-paid rugby league player in England," Shankland recalled years later. "Some people didn't like it. 'You've come over here to take our jobs,' a few said to me. 'Wrong,' I told them. 'I've come over here to teach you how to play'."

The club also lost two stalwarts during the campaign. Arthur Skelhorn, the former Warrington, Lancashire, England and Great Britain forward, died aged just 45, of bronchial pneumonia in April. In keeping with many past players,

'GAS' - George Arthur Skelhorn - had become a pub landlord when his playing days were over and was the licensee of the Hawthorn Hotel on Orford Lane.

Vice-president Thomas Pemberton, who had been the treasurer for 37 years until 1919, died aged 69 in October. Pemberton had been a prominent half-back for Padgate in his youth and played in the last match between Padgate and Warrington, in a field under the Three Arches, Slutchers Lane, before the clubs merged in 1881. He had also played for the newly merged Warrington club before taking on the treasurer's duties. He was also a magistrate and a partner in T. and J.L. Tunstall, the accountants and estate agents.

Wilderspool was once again chosen to stage a representative match, a County Championship clash between Lancashire and Cumberland on Saturday 4 October. The game pitted four Warrington players against each other. Lancashire centre Billy Dingsdale and hooker Nat Bentham found themselves on opposite sides to Cumberland full-back Billy Holding and scrum-half Bob Beattie in front of 10,000 fans. Dingsdale, always the man for the big occasion, scored two tries as Lancashire won 24-17 despite four goals from Holding.

The 1930-31 season also saw the end of one of the great Warrington careers, that of prop forward Billy Cunliffe. Cunliffe played twice in September but, after that, was unable to secure a place in the first team. Finally, and reluctantly, in December, he was transferred to Broughton Rangers so that he could continue playing. He had made 438 appearances for Warrington, scoring 38 tries and kicking six goals. He had won 11 Great Britain caps, 10 England caps and gone on two tours to Australia and New Zealand. He had also made 19 appearances for Lancashire. Like his former front-row colleague Arthur Skelhorn, he also ran a pub, the Black Bull Hotel at Lamberhead Green, Wigan.

A Wilderspool hero: Billy Holding

Rugby league between the wars was very different to rugby league today. For example, the first team and the 'A' team played at home on alternate Saturdays and, sometimes, the crowd watching the 'A' team play at Wilderspool was bigger than the crowd watching the first team play away. In addition, before the start of every season, an 'A' team captain was appointed and was a respected figure within the club.

The standard of play in 'A' team games was quite high too. All of which adds to Billy Holding's claims to be one of the greatest goalkickers and full-backs in the club's history. Not only did he kick 834 goals for the first team, he also kicked another 200 for the reserves, taking him well into four figures in the primrose and blue of Warrington, all kicked in the straight-on, toe-poke style of the day.

He was the first Warrington player to kick 100 goals in a season, a feat he managed in the 1930-31 campaign, and he once kicked a then club record 13 goals in an 'A' team match against Broughton Rangers 'A' at Wilderspool in October 1938.

He was also the first Warrington player to kick a goal at Wembley and, at Wigan in a Challenge Cup third round tie in March 1933, he kicked probably the greatest goal in the club's history.

By the end of that sensational 1932-33 season, he had stretched his club records to 125 goals and 256 points, records that stood until Harold Palin booted them into touch 16 years later. Yet there was much more to Holding's game than just goalkicking. His positional play was excellent as well and helped him to win 14 county caps for his native Cumberland. He was also a strong contender for the 1936 Great Britain tour of Australia and New Zealand until a broken leg at Leeds ended his season.

Holding, who started his Warrington career in March 1927 as a teenage trialist from Maryport with the pseudonym Kimberley, collected two Lancashire Cup winners' medals – in 1929 and 1932 – and would have collected a third in 1937 had he not woken up with tonsillitis on the morning of the final.

He was, of course, also an unfortunate victim of the 'So close to Glory' curse, playing in three major finals – the 1933 Challenge Cup Final, the 1935 Championship Final and the 1937 Championship Final – and finishing on the losing side each time.

At the end of his Warrington career, after a well-deserved testimonial season, he joined Rochdale Hornets. However, he returned to Wilderspool in November 1940 to make one final appearance, against St Helens, as a guest player, taking his appearance tally to an impressive 328. He also guested briefly for Salford before retiring in 1941.

After the war, however, he came out of retirement to make 19 appearances for the fledgling Workington Town club, kicking 31 goals and making his final appearance against Oldham in a Lancashire Cup tie in September 1946. In total, throughout his career, he had kicked 975 goals.

A measure of Holding's greatness was the fact his club record of 834 goals for Warrington remained in place until he was well into his seventies. It was not until January 1982, more than 40 years after he had last pulled on a primrose and blue jersey, that Steve Hesford took it from him. Holding died, aged 79, in November 1986.

Billy the Goalkicker: With apologies to Billy the Kid, *Warrington Guardian* cartoonist Gordon Roylance pays tribute to Billy Holding in February 1938. (Courtesy *Warrington Guardian*)

13. 1931-32: Shankland takes centre stage

Club president: Austin Crowe. Club captain: Billy Dingsdale.

Bill Shankland and Nelson Hardy arrived at Warrington's Bank Quay Station on Saturday 25 July and were greeted on the platform by club officials. As the party left the station a crowd of 300 supporters surged forward to see the new signings and then gave them a cheer as they were driven away. Warrington had never seen anything like it.

The pair began training every day and going on long runs to build up stamina. More than 5,000 fans turned up for the first practice match on Saturday 22 August when the first team took on the 'A' team. Another practice match the following Tuesday gave the committee a final chance to pick the team for the opening match of the season, at home to St Helens Recs.

The two Australians – or colonials, as they were often referred to – were paired together on the right flank and a crowd of 13,000 packed into Wilderspool to watch them in action. Shankland, on the right wing, scored his first try for the club five minutes from time. Taking a long pass from new captain Billy Dingsdale, he shrugged off a couple of would-be tacklers to force his way over in the corner. Full-back Billy Holding kicked the goal, his fifth of the match, to seal a 16-6 victory. Two days later, Shankland proved his all-round ability by winning a goalkicking competition at Widnes.

Shankland was an instant success. At Hull in October, he scored all of Warrington's points in a 7-7 draw. Playing at centre for the first time, he side-stepped and swerved his way through the Hull ranks for a try by the posts before adding the goal and kicking a penalty.

Restored to the wing in November, Shankland scored a hat-trick of tries in a 28-16 victory against Batley at Wilderspool. He was living up to all expectations. Try as he might, however, Hardy was struggling to make an impression and soon found himself relegated to the 'A' team.

Warrington were starting to rely on Shankland and when their super-fit Australian superstar was absent with flu at St Helens they crashed to a 38-8 defeat. The only bright spot of a miserable afternoon was the debut of local lad Jack Garrett on the left wing. He scored both Warrington tries.

One of Shankland's main reasons for coming to England was because he wanted to be a professional golfer and, in February, he was appointed assistant professional at West Lancashire Golf Club at Blundellsands. He celebrated his appointment with a spectacular try against Leigh at Wilderspool. Shankland stole the ball from Allan Houghton, the Leigh winger, and then set off along the touchline, eluding two tacklers to score in the corner. Warrington won 26-7.

Shankland was confident and competitive and those attributes earned him a sending off for retaliation in the final home game of the season. He had, however, already crossed for his 23rd and final try of the season.

Warrington made two other major signings during the season, the giant second-row forward Arthur 'Candy' Evans from Castleford and the highly rated winger Steve Ray from Wakefield. Evans had played rugby union and rugby league for Wales. He was 6 feet 3 inches tall and weighed 15 stones 10 pounds and had made his name at Pontypool in rugby union, winning three caps for Wales in 1924. He was also the amateur heavyweight boxing champion of Wales before going north to join Halifax in the 1924-25 season. Evans made his Wire debut against Bramley on Saturday 26 September and soon struck up a lasting friendship with Welsh scrum-half Dai Davies, acting as his minder on and off the pitch. Steve Ray arrived in January and would vindicate his signing with an impressive tally of 45 tries in 64 appearances over the next two years.

But the Warrington pack was still not as strong as the committee would have liked and so they planned an even more audacious signing, that of the Neath and Wales international rugby union forward Arthur Lemon, who had nine caps and worked in the Neath steelworks. Lemon, however, rejected their offer.

Warrington also gave an 'A' team trial to a young centre from the south of England who was given the pseudonym Whalley. The *Warrington Guardian*, in the politically incorrect style of those times, described him as "dark skinned".

Unfortunately, the lavish spending did not yield the expected results. Warrington only finished eighth in the league with 22 victories and 14 defeats and suffered second-round exits in the Lancashire and Challenge Cups, against Salford and Wakefield respectively.

Wilderspool was chosen to stage the County Championship match between Lancashire and Yorkshire in October and a crowd of 10,049 turned out to watch Lancashire win 11-8.

Rugby league was also moving with the times and the match between Warrington and Halifax at Wilderspool on 2 January 1932 became the first league fixture to be broadcast on the radio. Inevitably, Warrington lost 2-0.

In a move 64 years ahead of the formation of Super League and the game's move to a summer season, a letter from Warrington, St Helens, Leigh, Broughton Rangers and Salford asking for permission to arrange a summer competition in July and August was ruled out of order at a Rugby League Council meeting on March 21.

Warrington had also found themselves in conflict with the Rugby Football League over the staging of their most eagerly anticipated home fixture, against Wigan. The game was given a midweek date instead of a Saturday, when a bigger crowd could be expected and despite Warrington's protests, the League Committee refused to change it. The match went ahead on Wednesday 9 September and to the club's amazement attracted a crowd of 18,540, a then record for a league game at Wilderspool. Warrington had a great win, 12-8.

Bob Anderton, the Warrington secretary, was elected business manager of the Great Britain party to tour Australia and New Zealand and – after trial

The fab four: Top row: Hooker Nat Bentham, stand-off Jimmy Newcomb, forward Sammy Hardman; and on the left groundsman Tommy Flynn were all key figures at the club and so caught the eye of the *Warrington Guardian* cartoonist Pennington.
(Courtesy *Warrington Guardian*)

matches at Wilderspool and Headingley – captain Billy Dingsdale was selected to join him as one of the centres.

Dai Davies, who had played well all season and showed excellent form in the final trial at Leeds, was not so lucky. It seems that the selectors were wary of the Welshman's abrasive personality and willingness to confront authority. Full-back Billy Holding also played in the trials, but missed out on selection despite having kicked 102 goals during the season, 92 for Warrington and 10 for Cumberland.

The tourists set sail from Southampton on Wednesday 13 April with Anderton full of optimism for their prospects and full of praise for Jim Sullivan, the Wigan and Great Britain full-back and tour captain.

"It is good to know," said Anderton, "that on your side you have a man like Sullivan – one of the greatest players our game or any other game has ever known. Our side is going to have the Ashes when we return in September and, more than that, it is going to play the best of football in the fight to keep them. We have the men who can do it. Best of all, we are going to be one big happy family. The proof of that is there for all to see – the men are a team already. It could not be better."

During the summer, readers of the *Warrington Examiner* newspaper were able to follow Anderton's progress on the tour and learn that he had a most welcome visitor when he arrived in Auckland towards the end of the trip.

"The first person who came to see me was Bert Renwick, who used to play for Warrington," Anderton wrote. "He was wearing the Challenge Cup runner-up medal which he won when Huddersfield beat our team in the final at Leeds in 1913." Almost 20 years later, Renwick, who had captained the team that day, was still proud to have played in the famous primrose and blue of Warrington.

Like Bill Shankland, Arthur 'Candy' Evans had sporting ambitions away from rugby league. The giant Welshman wanted to be a successful, professional heavyweight boxer and, in May, fought Ireland's Jack Doyle at London's Crystal Palace, but the bout only lasted two minutes. After Evans had scored with two light lefts, the Irishman knocked him out with a heavy right to the jaw.

14. 1932-33: Wembley here we come

Club president: Austin Crowe. Club captain: Bill Shankland.

This was the season when full-back Billy Holding proved beyond all doubt that he was the greatest goalkicker the club had ever seen. The Cumbrian kicked a club record 125 goals, including perhaps the greatest goal in the club's history, and scored a club record 256 points. By any standards it was a successful campaign, with Warrington winning the Lancashire Cup and reaching their first Wembley Final. They also finished fifth in the league with the same number of points as third-placed York and fourth-placed Wigan, but missed out on the play-offs because of an inferior points record.

Under the inspirational captaincy of Australian Bill Shankland, Warrington beat Barrow, St Helens Recs and Wigan, all at Wilderspool, on their way to the Lancashire Cup Final. The 21-10 semi-final victory over Wigan, of course, gave rise to the most satisfaction and was achieved in magnificent style with all four members of the threequarter line, wingers Steve Ray and Tommy Thompson and centres Bill Shankland and Billy Dingsdale, scoring tries.

The Final against St Helens at Central Park attracted a crowd of 28,500 and they were treated to a thrilling match. Dai Davies scored the opening try under the posts, making it easy for Billy Holding to add the conversion, but St Helens fought back to lead 7-5 at half-time. A Holding penalty brought the scores level before a thrilling passing move along the Warrington backline created an overlap for Tommy Thompson to cross in the corner. Holding, for once, missed with the conversion and St Helens pulled two points back with a penalty goal to make the score 10-9, but the cup was Warrington's. The team returned home by coach and, after a drive through the main streets, they were served tea at a local cafe. They later received a civic reception at the town hall.

Leigh and Batley were swept aside in the opening rounds of the Challenge Cup to pave the way for a quarter-final at Wigan in March that was played out in front of a 38,000 crowd, including 15,000 from Warrington.

With time running out, Wigan were leading 7-4 when Dai Davies crossed in the corner to level the scores with the conversion attempt to come. Billy Holding teed up the ball almost on the touchline and, with the help of some spectators, made a pathway through the straw that had been used to protect the pitch from frost. It is difficult to imagine a more difficult and demanding kick.

The crowd fell silent as Holding ran up and toe-poked the ball, which sailed through the gathering gloom and between the posts for the most important goal of his career. It was Warrington's first win over Wigan at Central Park since December 1919, 14 years earlier, ending a run of 15 straight defeats. Two weeks later, Holding was at it again, kicking four more goals in the semi-final at Swinton to seal an 11-5 victory over St Helens and take Warrington to Wembley for the first time.

Warrington captain Bill Shankland takes the Lancashire Cup to Warrington Town Hall to show the Mayor, Councillor John Starkey. Also pictured, left to right, are Stan Jones (club treasurer), Arthur 'Candy' Evans, Jack 'Cod' Miller, Austin Crowe (club president) and Bob Anderton (club secretary)

Tickets went on sale the following week. Ground tickets 2/0d each; stand tickets, not numbered, 3/0d each and stand tickets, numbered, were 5/0d, 7/6d and 10/6d each.

Warrington fans were still celebrating when the next home game arrived, against Bradford Northern, and they were given something else to shout about as left winger Tommy Thompson became the first Wire player to score six tries in a match in an emphatic 38-12 victory. Billy Holding, of course, went one better by kicking seven goals.

Warrington also honoured two stalwarts of the previous decade, Frank Williams and Frank Mason, with a benefit match against Halifax in March. Both players had been born and bred in Warrington and had served the club with distinction, Williams making 352 first-team appearances and Mason 105. Each received £89/12/6.

Everything seemed to be going Warrington's way until they suffered two setbacks in the run-up to the Final. First, the former club president Fair Barber, a former Warrington captain, died at the end of April aged 58 after a long illness. Thomas Fairclough Barber, to give him his full name, had started his career with the Stockton Heath rugby club but when, in 1893, they disbanded he joined Warrington. He was the first-team captain in the 1895-96 season, the first following the breakaway from the Rugby Football Union, and went on to make 70 appearances for the fledgling rugby league club.

Barber's death was upsetting. But the next setback struck at the very heart of the team, with Welsh winger Steve Ray, Warrington's leading try scorer with a club record 33 in 44 matches, ruled out of the final with a septic thigh which required treatment in the borough General Hospital. Tommy Blinkhorn, the former Great Britain winger, was his replacement. It would be his 126th and final appearance for Warrington before he was transferred to Broughton Rangers for £100 in September.

The Final kicked off at 3.00pm but, from 2.15pm until 2.50pm, to get supporters in the mood, there was community singing conducted by T.P. Ratcliff, the *News Chronicle* song leader. Seventeen songs were on the song sheet: *My Girl's A Yorkshire Girl, Pack Up Your Troubles, Tipperary, She's A Lassie From Lancashire, For They Are Jolly Good Fellows, Abide With Me, Clementine, Daisy, Oh! The Noble Duke of York, There's A Long, Long, Trail, On Ilkley Moor Baht 'at, Loch Lomond, Cockles and Mussels, Smile, John Brown's Body, Boys Of The Old Brigade* and *Love's Old Sweet Song.*

1933 Challenge Cup Final

Warrington versus Huddersfield at Wembley Stadium on 6 May 1933.
Attendance: 41,874.

In keeping with the Challenge Cup Final's growing status since its move to London, the Rugby Football League had arranged for King George V to be the guest of honour. He was to be introduced to the teams beforehand and would present the trophy afterwards. The King, however, was unable to attend because of illness and so his son, Edward, the dashing Prince of Wales took his place.

The Prince's equerry visited the Warrington changing room before the match to spell out the protocol. "Captain Shankland," he said, "only speak if you are spoken to." Shankland said that he had already met the Prince once, in 1929. The equerry was not convinced or impressed and repeated: "Only speak if you are spoken to." Out on the pitch, before a record crowd, the Prince spotted the Warrington captain at the head of the line. "So Shankland, we meet again," said the Prince. "How's your golf?" "Fine sir," Shankland replied calmly. "How's yours?" Incidentally, Edward had already met the American divorcee Mrs Wallis Simpson and was set firmly on a path that would lead to him abdicating the throne in December 1936.

According to Shankland, some of the Warrington players were shaking with nerves in the changing room at Wembley before the match and that no doubt contributed to their nailbiting 21-17 defeat. Stand-off Jackie Oster, in particular, had a miserable afternoon, dropping a lot of passes and having a try near the posts controversially disallowed for a knock-on.

Publicity posters in London in the build-up to the final declared "Come to Wembley to see Holding the wonder goalkicker" but, on the big day, he was only successful with four attempts. Len Bowkett, the Huddersfield centre and captain, kicked six from six and that proved to be the difference between the teams.

Warrington, though, lost the match in the opening 20 minutes when they did not make the most of their chances. On two occasions the unfortunate Oster fumbled the ball when centres Bill Shankland and Billy Dingsdale were well placed.

Two penalty goals from Bowkett, after 20 and 25 minutes, gave Huddersfield a 4-0 lead before Fred Brindle, the Huddersfield loose-forward, crossed for the game's opening try and Bowkett again added the goal to make the score 9-0. Brindle, incidentally, was wearing a number 14 on his back, not a number 13, because Huddersfield thought that a number 13 would bring them bad luck.

They may have been right because it was at this point that Oster had his try disallowed, although he recovered his poise to send Billy Dingsdale running to the posts for Warrington's first try at Wembley which Billy Holding converted.

Two minutes before the break, scrum-half Dai Davies, who was easily Warrington's best player, darted over from a scrum close to the Huddersfield line and Holding again added the goal for a 10-9 lead.

Davies was clearly Warrington's danger man and so at half-time, as the teams went down the tunnel, Huddersfield loose-forward Fred Brindle tried to frighten him off. "I'll kill you in the second half," he said. "I'll twist you in two."

Davies was not worried or intimidated. He simply shouted across to his minder and room-mate, the 6 feet 3 inches Arthur 'Candy' Evans, a former boxer, for moral support. "Have you heard this fella Candy? He's going to kill me in the second half."

"I'll bloody kill him if he does anything to you," Evans reassured his fellow Welshman and the second half duly passed without any incidents of foul play.

After the break, Huddersfield regained the lead with Bowkett's third penalty goal before right winger Mills crossed for a try and Bowkett again converted to put the Yorkshire side 16-10 ahead.

Billy Holding cut the lead to four points with a penalty but, after 74 minutes, stand-off Gwyn Richards scored Huddersfield's third try and Bowkett did the rest for an almost unassailable 21-12 advantage. Dai Davies' second try, a carbon copy of the first and again improved by Holding, completed the scoring.

"We won, I think, because our backs took all their chances – even the thinnest of chances," said the victorious Bowkett. "Our forwards were beaten, although playing a most plucky game. Our superiority in pace was a great asset, both in attack and defence."

Bill Shankland agreed. "Huddersfield never missed any sort of a chance, and their pace aided them greatly in defence and recovery," he said. "Our forwards played a marvellous game, but we could not quite do the trick this time."

Both teams went to Brighton for a day out on the Sunday before returning home by train on the Monday. A crowd of 20,000, including many women and children, turned out to welcome Warrington home. Only 15,000 greeted Huddersfield. The players had a civic reception at the town hall and, after that, an evening at the Crown and Sceptre, Bob Anderton's pub.

It had been a season to remember and a record-breaking one, with Warrington beating Wigan four times and St Helens four times, a feat they had never achieved before. Both Lancashire rivals were defeated home and away in the league and in both cup competitions.

However, the final did have an unhappy postscript when Dai Davies, the Warrington scrum-half, found the Wembley match ball on display in an off licence belonging to J. Canon Bardsley, a Conservative councillor and one of the club's committee men. Davies was furious. He borrowed the ball, never took it back and pinned the unfortunate Bardsley up against the door of the committee room when he demanded its return. It was not the most sensible thing he had ever done.

Warrington: W.J. Holding, T. Thompson, W. Dingsdale, W.J. Shankland, T. Blinkhorn, J. Oster, D.M. Davies, J. Miller, N. Bentham, S. Hardman, A. Evans, R. Smith, C. Seeling jnr.

Huddersfield: T. Scourfield, E. Mills, S. Brogden, L.C. Bowkett, R. Markham, G. Richards, L. Adams, H. Sherwood, C. Halliday, T. Banks, H. Tiffany, E. Talbot, F. Brindle.

Referee: F. Fairhurst (Wigan).

Warrington had chartered a special dining train to take hundreds of supporters to Wembley and the train left Euston Station at 12.25am on Sunday morning for the return journey to Bank Quay. Supper was served 15 minutes later with the menu as follows: thick mock turtle soup followed by hot roast lamb with mint sauce, green vegetables and baked and boiled potatoes. The dessert was biscuits, cheese, watercress and butter. There was no vegetarian option but then, in those days, vegetarians were rare. The train arrived back in Warrington at 4.40am. A long and historic day was over.

The Warrington team who beat St Helens in the semi-final, pictured at Wilderspool. Left to right, back: Nat Bentham, Bob Smith, Arthur Evans, Charlie Seeling, Sammy Hardman, Jack Miller. Middle: Steve Ray, Billy Dingsdale, Bill Shankland (captain), Tommy Thompson, Billy Holding. Front: Jackie Oster & Dai Davies.

Left: Showing a clean pair of heels: Secretary Bob Anderton and trainer Billy Bennett inspect the players' boots at Wembley on the eve of the big match.

Below: Warrington's Challenge Cup Final team as featured in the Wembley programme. (Courtesy Alan Domville & RFL)

Left: The Wembley programme (Courtesy Alan Domville & RFL)
Right: Bill Shankland makes a break at Wembley.

Warrington players do some sprint work in the build-up to the big game.

No try! Billy Holding appeals in vain to the referee at Wembley watched by team-mates Tommy Blinkhorn (centre) and Bill Shankland. Gwyn Richards' touchdown was given. Huddersfield's Stan Brogden (right) looks on.

Heading for the line: Dai Davies scoring one of his two tries at Wembley.

Right Royal Rugby: Gannon, the *Daily Dispatch's* cartoonist, captures the magic of the 1933 Final. Fred Brindle, the Huddersfield loose-forward, wore a No14 jersey while Warrington's No13, Charlie Seeling, finished the match with a black eye.

A Wilderspool hero: Dai Davies

Is a glass half full or half empty? Was Warrington's Welsh scrum-half Dai Davies lucky to appear in four Challenge Cup Finals (1928, 1933, 1935 and 1937), or unlucky to finish on the losing side every time?

Only he could answer that question, of course, but he was certainly proud of his seven years as a Warrington player, so proud in fact that he was still wearing his club blazer decades later. And he could be equally proud of his half-back partnership with fellow Welshman Tommy Flynn which is still regarded as one of the best combinations in the club's history.

Warrington signed Davies from Broughton Rangers in November 1927 for £650 after a week of haggling between the two clubs over the size of the fee. He quickly proved his worth and played in his first Challenge Cup Final, against Swinton at Central Park, five months later.

His best performance in primrose and blue came on the biggest stage of all, Wembley, when he scored two tries in the thrilling 1933 final against Huddersfield. Both came straight from scrums close to the line and were a tribute to his lightning acceleration.

That match can be seen as the beginning of the end of his time at Warrington, because it led to the clash with J. Canon Bardsley outlined earlier. Warrington signed another scrum-half, Jack Goodall, the following year and Davies, by now aged 31, was sold to Huddersfield where he collected his third Challenge Cup Final losers' medal. His fourth, as the Keighley captain, followed in 1937.

While at Wilderspool, Davies won four caps for Wales and collected a Lancashire Cup winners' medal after scoring a try in the 1932 Final against St Helens.

Davies died, aged 89, in February 1992 and a wonderful book about his career *Man of Amman – The Life of Dai Davies*, written by Phil Melling, was published in 1994.

A local hero: Sunny Lowry (Anderson)

Three months after Warrington's first Wembley Final in 1933, a 22-year-old woman named Sunny Lowry entered the record books in her own right when she swam the English Channel.

It was Sunny's third attempt at the swim and, after being thwarted first time by jellyfish and second time by a severe storm, she was more determined than ever. Her successful attempt began at Cap Gris Nez, near Calais, in France on the evening of 28 August when she was covered in lanolin to protect her from the cold and waded into the water. Again she encountered jellyfish but, sustained only by drinks of coffee, cocoa and beef tea, she emerged at St Margaret's Bay, Dover, 15 hours and 41 minutes later.

She was only the seventh woman and 15th swimmer overall to conquer the world-famous waterway. The distance, as the crow flies, was 21 miles but the vagaries of the tides made the swim much longer.

"I really fancied a steak afterwards but could not eat properly because my mouth was swollen from being in the sea water for so long," recalled Sunny, aged 96, in 2007. "All I could manage was porridge."

The swim was a triumph for hard work, tenacity and the world's first bikini: "I made my own two-piece swimsuit out of cotton rather than wool," she said. "Once when I came out of the water at Margate after training I was showing a bit of midriff and a woman said she would report me to the police. So my trainer told me to pull my trunks up and my top down each time I came out of the water so as not to show any flesh."

Years of training had paid off: "I saw a little advert in a paper," Sunny explained. "A German coach wanted a British girl to swim the Channel. It was always one of my ambitions and I jumped at the chance. My father had the money to support my attempts, he was a fish and poultry dealer, and stood behind me and my ambitions. So I moved away from home for the first time to train.

"The final preparations involved me swimming in Dover Harbour for six months from March to August. It was full-time training and I was put through a rigorous keep fit and diet programme.

"I went from 9 stone 3 pounds to 14 stone 7 pounds and built up my muscles with medicine ball push-ups and press gripping rubber handlebar grips. My main diet was eggs, 40 a week, including eight-egg omelettes. I also went for long walks to get used to being alone in the water."

Sunny's first attempt ended when she was pulled from the water unconscious after being stung by jellyfish. Her second attempt was even more heartbreaking after she lost touch with the support boat.

"I was so unlucky in my second," she said. "There was a storm and they lost me just off Folkestone. It was only for a flash of lightning and them seeing my

Sunny Lowry swimming the English Channel in August 1933.

red cap that saved me. They circled me in the boat and flashed me which indicated the swim was abandoned. I shouted to them 'My father's put a lot of money into this and I'm not coming out,' but they threw a towel to touch my head which meant it was all over."

The third attempt more than made up for that disappointment and Sunny's two-piece costume is now on display at the Cross Channel Museum in Dover.

The Channel swim was a remarkable achievement but formed only one chapter in a lifelong love of the sport. When she was 30, Sunny, from Manchester, married Bill Anderson and settled in Warrington. Over the course of the next 30 years, they taught hundreds of local children how to swim – and how to swim better.

In 1964, they were both founder members of the Warrington Dolphins Long Distance Swimming Club, which is still going strong and presents a trophy in their honour.

In 2001, aged 90, Sunny was installed as president of the Channel Swimming Association at their annual meeting at the Webbs Hotel, Dover. She also became a keen supporter of the campaign to restore Manchester's Victoria Baths, where she had learned to swim at the age of seven in 1918, to its former glory.

In 2003, aged 92 and 70 years after her epic Channel swim, she was still swimming once a week at Fordton Leisure Centre. She also met the Prince of Wales. In 2005, she was awarded the MBE for services to swimming.

Sunny, who was born in Longsight in 1911, attended Manchester High School for Girls and is hailed as a "shining example" on their website: "Sunny Lowry is a wonderful role model for the current generation of Manchester High School girls and shows that there is nothing you cannot achieve once you set your mind to it." Even swimming the Channel.

Sunny Lowry died, aged 97, on Wednesday 20 February 2008.

15. 1933-34: Vive la France

Club president: Austin Crowe. Club captain: Bill Shankland.

For almost 40 years rugby league had been trying to expand its horizons beyond its narrow northern heartland, with varying degrees of success and those efforts continued in the 1933-34 season, with Warrington very much at the centre of things. Wilderspool hosted games against Australia and France while Warrington played in London and Dublin.

The Australians were making their fifth Kangaroo tour and stopped off twice at Wilderspool. Their first visit, in September, attracted a crowd of 16,576 for the match against a Lancashire team featuring Warrington centre Billy Dingsdale and second-row forward Bob Smith. Australia won comfortably, 33-7, with centre Dave Brown, who would later join Warrington, kicking six goals and scoring two tries.

While still a teenager, Brown had lost all his hair after contracting a virus when swimming. To cover his embarrassment, and his head, he wore a wig. Nobody was fooled, however, and on the boat to England, one of his team-mates, unable to stand the sight of the hairpiece any longer, tossed it out of one of the ship's portholes. After that, Brown started wearing a distinctive skullcap when playing and that became his trademark.

Warrington avenged that defeat the following month with a 15-12 victory, thanks to two tries from second-row forward Arthur 'Candy' Evans in front of another 16,000-plus crowd. The Australian forward Ray Stehr, a Sydney policeman back home, was sent off for foul play just before half-time, while Bill Shankland, the Warrington captain, produced an excellent display against his fellow countrymen.

After the match, the Kangaroos needed three cabin trunks to carry away all the presents – seven for each member of the tour party – they had been given by the club and local businesses. Each member of the party received the following: cufflinks from the Warrington club; 100 cigarettes from Fletcher, Russell and company; a pearl pocket knife and case from brewers Greenall Whitley; a leather wallet and pencil from Mr Tom Gibbons of Manchester; a gold-plated Wardonia safety razor and blades in a case from T. Ward and Sons Ltd and erasmic toilet soaps from J. Crosfield and Sons. The Kangaroos of 1933, unlike the highly-paid athletes of today, were ordinary working men – for a start, most of them smoked – and were overjoyed at the club's and the town's hospitality.

At 9pm, following a post-match banquet, the Australians boarded their charabanc and set off to Blackpool to see the illuminations, staying there until the lights were switched off at midnight. They finally arrived back at the team hotel, the Marlborough House at Ilkley in Yorkshire, at 3.30am on Sunday.

The next foreign visitors to Warrington were from closer to home. France had been expelled from rugby union's Five Nations Championship for professionalism and violent play, so one of their leading players, Jean Galia, organised a six-match rugby league tour of England. It concluded with their first representative fixture, against a Rugby League XIII at Wilderspool on Saturday 17 March.

The French team were treated to a civic reception at the town hall beforehand and each member of the side was presented with a pewter ash tray emblazoned with the Warrington coat of arms in enamel and inscribed with the player's name. The Rugby League XIII, including Warrington scrum-half Dai Davies, however, were too experienced for the French novices and won 32-16 in front of 11,000 fans. After the final whistle, the players formed a circle and, with the crowd joining in, sang *Auld Lang Syne*.

Rugby league was also trying to conquer London and so the Wigan Highfield club was reborn as London Highfield, playing at the White City Stadium. The experiment lasted just one season, but was long enough for Warrington to make two trips to the capital, a more expensive outing than their normal away fixtures. The first, on Wednesday 6 December, was for a league game with an 8pm kick-off, making it the first time Warrington had played under floodlights and with a white ball. Steve Donoghue and his friend Gordon Richards, another leading jockey, were there to cheer the Wire on. It was a bitterly cold night and braziers were positioned around the ground to keep supporters warm. The floodlights were said to be the equivalent of 40 million candles and lit up the pitch without casting a single shadow. Under these conditions, Billy Holding, the Warrington full-back, had no trouble seeing the ball and did not miss a single catch all night. Warrington won 15-5 and, three days later, won the return league match 8-5 at Wilderspool.

Come February, Warrington were drawn away to London in the second round of the Challenge Cup. Because most Warrington fans were unable to make the journey south, the club booked a telephone line for two hours, linking White City to Wilderspool, to provide supporters at that afternoon's 'A' team game against St Helens with updates. The novelty of it all attracted a crowd of 8,000 to Wilderspool and the plan worked perfectly in every respect, except that Warrington lost 19-5. It almost goes without saying that stand-off Jackie Oster, who had had such a miserable time in the 1933 Challenge Cup Final and had been transferred from Warrington to Highfield the previous month, was in inspirational form against his former club.

Oster was replaced in the Warrington squad by the 23-year-old Welshman Ben Hawker, who was signed from Cross Keys RUFC. A target for several leading rugby league clubs, Hawker agreed terms with Warrington officials on the evening of Friday 29 December. He then travelled all night before making his Warrington debut, against Halifax at Wilderspool, the following afternoon. Hawker deputised for half-back Dai Davies, who was playing for Wales against Australia at Wembley. Hawker's terms were: a signing-on fee of £250 and the promise of a weekly wage of £3/10/0 for the next three years.

Councillor Austin Crowe, the Mayor of Warrington and club president, opened the new changing rooms under the main stand before Warrington played Hull on 13 January 1934. Bill Shankland is the Warrington captain.

Warrington, however, were disappointing in the league with 22 victories and 15 defeats, leaving them in eighth place, although there were some notable highlights, including a league double over Wigan. Warrington won 22-6 at Wilderspool on the opening day of the season when full-back Billy Holding kicked five goals and then secured a 9-6 win at Central Park in October when stand-off Jimmy Newcomb scored a try and kicked a drop goal. Those two victories meant that Warrington had now beaten Wigan six times in a row. Billy Holding finished the season with 116 goals, the fourth year in a row he had reached three figures.

As usual Warrington were also investing in the facilities at Wilderspool. New changing rooms under the main stand, built by Messrs Harry Fairclough at a cost of £700 and as good as any in the league, were officially opened by Councillor Austin Crowe, the Mayor of Warrington and club president, on 13 January 1934. The team followed the ceremony with a 16-8 victory over Hull. Until then there had been a wooden changing room hut at the Fletcher Street end, with the players entering the pitch through a gap in the wall. The hut also had another function: it opened down at the front to double as a refreshment kiosk.

For the players to reach the pitch from the new changing rooms, a tunnel had to be built under the stand. Fortunately, the club had plenty of former miners on the staff, notably groundsman Tommy Flynn, the former stand-off, and three current players in hooker Nat Bentham, scrum-half Dai Davies and full-back Billy Holding. The four of them duly obliged, although the tunnel soon flooded and remained a problem for years to come.

Warrington were also unlucky with their major signing of the season, Jack (J.T.) Woods, Barrow's Lancashire and Great Britain winger, who cost £600. Woods, aged 26, was 5 feet 10 inches tall and weighed 12 stones 7 pounds, and had twice toured Australia and New Zealand with Great Britain. He made seven consecutive appearances in February and March, scoring two tries against Batley, but then suffered an accident at work when he slipped off a scaffold, injuring his leg and spraining his back. He was ordered to rest by his doctor and missed the rest of the season.

However, the investment in facilities reaped an impressive dividend in May when Wilderspool was chosen to host the Championship Final between Wigan and Salford. As hosts, Warrington also produced the official match programme. Every programme was numbered and, at half-time, the winning number was shown on the scoreboard and its owner received five shillings from Bob Anderton, the club's honorary secretary, after the match. The Final attracted Wilderspool's first 30,000-plus crowd – 31,564, including 1,900 seated in the stand – and generated record receipts of £2,117. Inevitably, Wigan won 15-3.

Still, Warrington's pioneering season was not over. On 12 May 1934 they played Wigan at Shelbourne Park, Dublin, for the Irish Hospitals Trust Cup in the first game of rugby league to be played on Irish soil. A crowd of 10,000 attended – way below expectations – and, according to one press report, "marvelled at the speed and open nature of the play even on ground which was hard as iron". Fittingly, after such a disappointing season, Warrington lost 32-19.

As ever in rugby league, there was controversy over the Dublin match. After Warrington and Wigan had agreed to play "the first rugby league game in Ireland", Shelbourne Football Club invited Oldham to play Rochdale Hornets at the same venue on 28 April, two weeks earlier. Warrington and Wigan protested and the emergency committee of the Rugby League Council, meeting in Leeds, refused to sanction the Oldham versus Rochdale game.

Other signings during the season included scrum-half Len Galloway, winger Fred Simcock and Irish loose-forward Tom Griffin. Galloway, aged 20, who was signed from Saddleworth Rangers ARLFC at the beginning of March, had already scored 30 tries and 70 goals that season, which was believed to be a record for junior rugby league. He never made the grade at Wilderspool, however, and did not make a single first-team appearance.

Simcock, aged 21, was signed from Castner-Kellner RUFC at the end of March. He received £75 with the promise of another £25 after he had made six first-team appearances and a further £25 at Christmas if his form warranted it.

At 6 feet tall and weighing 12 stones 6 pounds, Simcock was a powerful runner and was handed his first-team debut against Swinton on 2 April. His early promise faded, however, and after three tries in 10 appearances he was transferred to Widnes for £60. Griffin, too, did not enjoy a long career in the primrose and blue. After signing from St Helens, he made just 15 first-team appearances, scoring two tries.

Among the former Warrington players who died during the season was John Eden, who died aged 58 in February. Eden was a local lad who played as a forward in the club's first Challenge Cup Final, against Batley at Headingley in 1901. Altogether, he had made 96 first-team appearances, scoring 10 tries.

Relations between rugby's two codes were as strained as ever. The Warrington programme for the match against Keighley in November carried an extract from the *Daily Express* under the pointed headline of "Still an Amateur". It read: "A rugby union player who travels 16 miles to play for a certain team has had his personal expenses increased from £5 to £8 because he had been offered £350 by a rugby league club to turn professional." The practice that became known as shamateurism was clearly alive and well.

A Wilderspool hero: Bill Shankland

Bill Shankland was, quite simply, the greatest all-round sportsman ever to play for Warrington and produced world-class performances in two professional sports – rugby league and golf.

He was also outstanding at rugby union, swimming, boxing, cricket and athletics. "I was lucky with my sport," said Shankland in an interview to mark his 90th birthday in 1997. "I could do anything. I was a very athletic chap."

As a young man, he boxed and swam for Australia, once taking on the great American swimmer Johnny Weissmuller, who later achieved fame and fortune as Tarzan in the cinema. He also found time to excel at cricket – he played with the great Don Bradman – and athletics.

As a rugby union fly-half, he toured New Zealand, South Africa and the British Isles during the 1926-27 season. Three years later he was back as a rugby league centre and one of the leading lights of that Kangaroo tour.

British rugby league clubs were desperate to sign him and, when he joined Warrington in 1931, he became one of the highest-paid players in the game. At Wilderspool, however, he proved to be worth every penny and became the first overseas player to captain a side at Wembley in a Challenge Cup Final – an honour he achieved against Huddersfield in 1933.

In total, he played in four major finals in four different positions – centre in the 1933 Challenge Cup Final, stand-off in the 1935 Championship Final, full-back in the 1936 Challenge Cup Final and winger in the 1937 Championship Final. He also collected two Lancashire Cup winners' medals, as captain in 1932 and as a key member of Jack Arkwright's team five years later.

His 231st and final appearance for Warrington ended in defeat against Widnes at Wilderspool on Good Friday 1938. But supporters were able to give him a proper send off when he was invited to kick off the home game against Widnes that November before starting his new job as a golf professional with Leeds City Council. Shankland was given a wonderful reception by the 16,000-strong crowd and, this time, Warrington won 7-5.

The Wire also benefited from his judgement of a rugby player as well. In 1945, he recommended that Warrington take a look at a young Australian winger by the name of Brian Bevan. The club agreed and was rewarded with a world record 740 tries in 620 appearances.

After finishing playing rugby league, he concentrated on his other love, golf, finishing joint third at the 1939 Open at St Andrews. He came even closer to lifting the Claret Jug at Royal Liverpool in 1947. Coming down the back nine in the last round he was in a fine position to win the tournament, until he hit a bunker at the 16th, took a six and finished fourth – two shots behind the champion, Fred Daly. Four years later, at Portrush, Northern Ireland, he was in contention again but tied for sixth place, eight shots behind the winner, Max Faulkner.

As the golf professional at the Potters Bar club in Middlesex he moulded the career of a brash, young Tony Jacklin, who became the Open champion in 1969. "Unquestionably, being there with Shanko probably made me," said Jacklin. "I couldn't have had a better grounding. It was like doing my National Service, which I never had to do. It hardened me, it really did, but I wouldn't like to go through it again."

Shankland was at Potters Bar for more than 20 years and helped to raise more than £200,000 for charity by pioneering pro-am tournaments. He eventually retired to Poole in Dorset and even in his 80s was still playing golf a couple of times a week, and getting round in less than his age.

Shankland made his last appearance at Wilderspool in September 1998, aged 91, as the star turn in a parade of past players to mark the ground's centenary. Tragically, at his hotel the following day, he slipped and fell, banging his head and never regaining consciousness. In 2003, he was made a founder member of the club's Hall of Fame.

Warrington legend Bill Shankland

The French visit to Wilderspool

Wilderspool staged French rugby league's first representative fixture when they took on a Rugby League XIII in March 1934. Bert Wright, the *Liverpool Evening Express's* cartoonist, recorded the occasion.

Warrington secretary Bob Anderton with Jean Galia, one of the founders of French rugby league. (Photo: Courtesy Robert Gate)

16. 1934-35: The idols of the town

Club president: Dr James Bennett. Club captain: Bill Shankland.

Warrington made two significant signings in July 1934, winger Griff Jenkins and second-row forward Rex King. Jenkins, son of the Welsh scrum-half Jack Jenkins who had played for Warrington from 1906 to 1910, was the first. He was snapped up from Weston-Super-Mare RUFC and had played for Somerset the previous season, scoring two tries against Kent. He received a £200 signing-on fee and a guaranteed wage of £3 per week, irrespective of whether the club could find him a suitable job outside rugby. Jenkins had, in fact, been born in Mersey Street, Warrington, but had grown up in the Rhondda Valley.

King, from the Canterbury rugby union club in New Zealand, was the next to arrive and went on to play in all 43 games during the season, scoring 16 tries. King, aged 24, had been a member of the Canterbury side who had beaten the British Lions during their 1930 tour and had been tipped to play for the All Blacks, but he wanted to come to England to complete his studies as a teacher. While at university, he had toured Australia with the New Zealand University union team. Warrington were so impressed with King that they returned to the Canterbury club at the end of October to sign half-back Roy Hazelhurst. A crowd of 5,000 turned out to see Hazelhurst, who was 5 feet 9 inches and 11 stones 8 pounds, make his debut for the 'A' team against Keighley 'A' at Wilderspool at the start of November.

Players were being moved on as well. Scrum-half Billy Kirk was controversially transferred to Liverpool Stanley in August after seven successful years with the club during which time he had scored 16 tries in 102 appearances. Popular wingers Tommy Thompson and Steve Ray were also sold, to Oldham for a joint fee of £400. Inevitably, after scoring 112 tries for Warrington, Thompson scored against them when the sides drew 7-7 at Watersheddings in September.

It was a time of transition at Wilderspool and results in the opening part of the season reflected that. Warrington won at Barrow on the opening day and beat Broughton Rangers in the first home game, but were thrashed 21-0 by Wigan in the league and 23-5 by Salford in the second round of the Lancashire Cup. Both those matches were played at Wilderspool and the supporters were getting restless.

Warrington beat Featherstone Rovers 24-3 in their next home game but not before some supporters had, unusually, barracked members of their own team. The committee realised that something had to be done to strengthen the side and were rightly pleased with themselves when they signed the giant second-row forward Jack Arkwright from St Helens for £700 in September. He was already 32 years old but, at 6 feet 3 inches tall and 16 stones, he proved to be a mighty addition to the pack.

Another major signing followed in October when scrum-half Jack Goodall was plucked from Nuneaton RUFC in exchange for a £350 signing-on fee to replace

Dai Davies. He was 23 years old, 5 feet 8 inches, 10 stones 10 pounds and had played for Warwickshire. He made his debut against Leigh at Wilderspool on 10 November and settled in quickly. Including his debut, Goodall made 66 consecutive appearances before missing a match. At last, the new-look Warrington team was beginning to take shape.

From that Leigh game until the end of the season, Warrington played 28 league games, winning 24, drawing one and losing only three to finish second in the final table with a club record 59 points. Warrington won nine games in a row in December and January, with the ninth victory - a 13-3 triumph against Leeds in front of a 19,000 Headingley crowd - being the most impressive of all. Warrington scored three tries that afternoon, through Jack Garrett, Griff Jenkins and Rex King.

Northern Rugby League - top of the table

	P	W	D	L	F	A	Pts
Swinton	38	30	1	7	468	175	61
Warrington	38	28	3	7	445	253	59
Wigan	38	26	4	8	790	290	56
Salford	38	27	1	10	478	272	55

In the Championship semi-final at Wilderspool, Warrington were up against their arch rivals Wigan, and a crowd of 23,484 packed into Wilderspool to watch the action. A desperate forward battle ensued which Warrington won 9-0 thanks to a try from scrum-half Jack Goodall, two goals from full-back Billy Holding and a drop goal from stand-off Jimmy Newcomb enabling them to reach their second Championship Final.

1935 Championship Final
Warrington versus Swinton at Central Park, Wigan, 11 May 1935.
Attendance: 27,700.

Nat Bentham was one of the best hookers ever to play for Warrington. Strong, rugged and resourceful, he had won 10 Great Britain caps and played for England and Lancashire. He had announced that the 1935 Championship Final would be his 202nd and last appearance for the Wire before retiring. He deserved to go out on a high note. Instead, the opposite occurred. He was sent off four minutes from time and the 12 men of Warrington lost the match 14-3.

On the day, everything went wrong. Warrington even lost the toss and so had to play into a glaring sun in the first half. They were then penalised at a scrum after 11 minutes and man-of-the-match Martin Hodgson, the Swinton second-row forward, kicked the first of four goals to make the score 2-0.

Swinton increased their lead five minutes before half-time when stand-off Dick Green crossed for a try and Hodgson added the conversion to make it 7-0.

Warrington's best spell came at the start of the second half when centre Billy Dingsdale, their best player on the day, scored their only try. Centre Ben Hawker broke through the Swinton defence and found winger Jack Garrett in support. Garrett dashed down the wing until he was tackled but still managed to get an inside pass away to Dingsdale. Full-back Billy Holding missed the conversion.

Hodgson kicked his third goal on the hour before Holding was carried off injured. He soon returned to the fray and Warrington redoubled their efforts but could find no more gaps in Swinton's strong defence.

Swinton sealed their victory four minutes from time when loose-forward Sullivan went over from a scrum near the line and Hodgson again added the goal. Towards the end, players on both sides lost their heads and Bentham was sent off for striking Bryn Evans, the Swinton scrum-half. A spectator rushed onto the pitch and was removed by the police.

Griff Jenkins drawn by Pennington, the *Warrington Guardian* cartoonist.

After the match, the Warrington team were honoured with a civic reception at the town hall, followed by the inevitable tea at Carter's Cafe. It was a time to drown sorrows.

Warrington: W.J. Holding, J.W. Garrett, A.B. Hawker, W. Dingsdale, G. Jenkins, W.J. Shankland, P.J. Goodall, S. Hardman, N. Bentham, J. Miller, J. Arkwright, R. King, J. Chadwick.

Swinton: R. Scott, J. McGregor, A. Hickman, H. Evans, F. Buckingham, R. Green, B. Evans, J. Wright, T. Armitt, G. Hughes, M. Hodgson, F. Beswick, J. Sullivan.
Referee: F Peel (Bradford).

Other players who moved on during the season included second-row forward Arthur 'Candy' Evans to Halifax and scrum-half Dai Davies to Huddersfield for £250. Nelson Hardy also returned home to Australia after his unhappy spell with the club.

Davies may have left Warrington, but he had not left his bad luck behind. He had already lost two Challenge Cup Finals with the Wire in 1928 and 1933, and was destined to lose two more, the 1935 match with Huddersfield and the 1937 match with Keighley whom he captained. So he played at Wembley for three different clubs and lost each time. While at Wilderspool, he also played at Wembley on two more occasions – for Wales against Australia in January 1930 and again in December 1933 – and suffered two more defeats. Still, he had no regrets about playing in the famous primrose and blue of Warrington.

"I never regretted signing for Warrington," said Davies in his biography. "They treated me well. There was no soccer team, only rugby in Warrington, and the rugby union team was nil. They all came to watch us – we were the idols of the town."

In the 1934-35 season, at least, that was perfectly understandable as Warrington won 21 out of their final 23 league games. It was a different story in the Challenge Cup. Before the first-round tie against Hull at Wilderspool, a new club flag was unfurled. Donated by a supporter, Sydney H. Davies, from Lymm, the flag was made up of two primrose and two blue quarters and bore the letters WRFC. It did not prove inspirational, the match finished in an 11-11 draw and Warrington lost the replay 16-2.

In March, Warrington were also presented with a new set of jerseys by supporter Harold Ward of T.W. Ward and Son (Wardonia) Ltd of Suez Street, Warrington. They were tangerine with a royal blue collar and cuffs and a primrose and blue W across the front.

Thanks to generosity of that kind, Warrington made a profit of £348 on the season, enough to sign another top quality player for the next campaign, and the 23,385 who packed into Wilderspool for the Wigan game in September set a club record home crowd for a league game.

There was also a French flavour to the season. Villeneuve, captained by Jean Galia, had opened their tour of England at Wilderspool in September while full-back Bill Baxter, Warrington's 'A' team skipper, had captained a 16-man Northern Rugby League squad on a three-match tour to France in January. The Northern Rugby League XIII won all three games – against Lyons, South East France and Roanne. Warrington secretary Bob Anderton accompanied the trip and even refereed the games against Lyons and Roanne. Baxter really entered into the French spirit. Before each match, as captain, he was presented with a bouquet of flowers and gracefully kissed, on both cheeks, the young girls who made the presentations.

Sadly, the club lost two stalwarts during the season. Harry Ashton, the former captain, secretary and president, died aged 74 in December at home at the Orford Hotel. He had captained the first Warrington team to win a trophy, the 1885-86 side who had lifted the South West Lancashire and Border Towns Cup by beating Aspull at Liverpool. Jacky Parker, who had been associated with the club for more than 45 years and served as the groundsman for 25, passed away aged 69 in September. A minute's silence in his honour was observed before the game against York on 6 October.

Amateur rugby league was flourishing in the town. The Warrington Ship Canal team became the first local junior side to reach the first round proper of the Challenge Cup, where they were defeated 28-9 by Dewsbury.

17. 1935-36: Wembley again

Club president: Dr James Bennett. Club captain: Bill Shankland.

Jack Arkwright was the Adrian Morley of his day: a Great Britain international, a powerhouse forward, a leader of men and, sometimes, a magnet for trouble. Arkwright was at his belligerent best – or worst – in Warrington's Lancashire Cup first round tie at Swinton, which ended in a 2-2 draw, and the replay, which the Wire won 14-8.

The Lancashire County Committee even held an inquiry into the rough play and concluded that the referees, J.E. Taylor and Frank Peel, could have taken firmer action, despite the fact that Peel sent three players off, including Arkwright and Jack Chadwick from Warrington. Arkwright was banned up to and including 30 November and so missed 10 matches. Chadwick was banned for four matches.

Arkwright, however, knew the game inside out and was becoming an important figure at the club. In November he recommended to the committee that they return to his former club, St Helens, and sign hooker Dave Cotton. The committee did as they were told and never regretted their decision. Cotton would go on to play for the club for the next 13 years, making 326 appearances and proved to be a master of his craft.

Loose-forward Bill Chapman had already been signed from Bridgend in August following a chance meeting with Dai Davies, the former Warrington scrum-half, in a Blackpool pub. Chapman was on holiday with some friends and Davies, recognising a familiar Welsh accent, introduced himself. Chapman said he was running out of money and so Davies offered to give him a loan if he agreed to play a trial match for Warrington. Chapman accepted the offer, impressed in the pre-season game and signed a contract. He was an important recruit, was 22 years old, 5 feet 10 inches tall and weighed 12 stones 10 pounds. He went on to play 179 games for the first team.

Warrington made another major signing in September when they recruited full-back Freddie French from the Canterbury rugby union club in New Zealand that had already supplied loose-forward Rex King and half-back Roy Hazelhurst. At 6 feet 2 inches and 14 stones 3 pounds, French was a well-known athlete in New Zealand, having won the national discus championship in 1932, 1933 and 1934 and the national javelin championship in 1933 and 1934.

French was met in London by Bob Anderton while King and Hazelhurst were waiting for the pair at Bank Quay Station. The signing generated great interest and 5,000 turned out to see French make his first appearance in a Warrington shirt for the 'A' team against Wigan 'A' at Wilderspool. Warrington won 13-0 but French was hurt early in the second half and ended up in Warrington Infirmary where an X-ray revealed a small fracture under his right eye and ruled him out for a month.

At the start of October, Warrington travelled to London to face the new Streatham and Mitcham club at Mitcham Stadium for a game that attracted a crowd of 18,000 and ignited hopes that rugby league would take off in the capital. Warrington won 17-7 but, before Christmas, had conceded a league double to Liverpool Stanley who were enjoying an excellent season.

Warrington lost 5-0 at Prescott Road on the day that Wilderspool was staging the Lancashire Cup Final between Salford, who had beaten Warrington, and Wigan. Billy Kirk, the former Warrington scrum-half, scored Stanley's only try, provoking another debate about whether Warrington had been right to sell him in the first place.

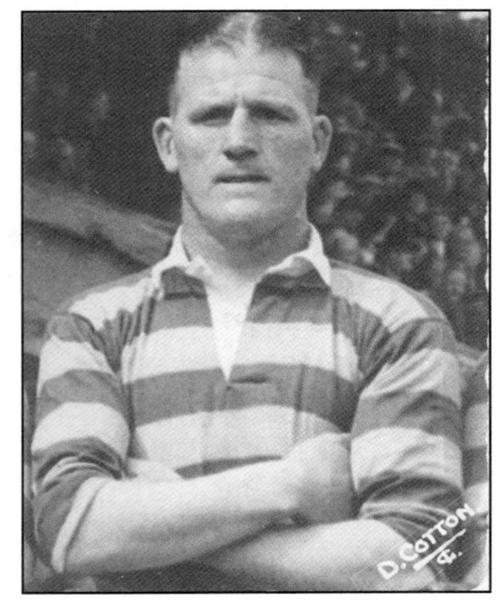

Dave Cotton
(Courtesy Stan Lewandowski)

Supporters, of course, are never happy for long, although Warrington did open the new year with six wins in a row, including an 18-7 victory at Leigh which was preceded by two minutes' silence for the late King George V.

By now, Challenge Cup fever was starting to grip Warrington and the Wire went on to reach their second Wembley Final in three years, although the run there stretched their playing resources to the limit, particularly in the full-back and goalkicking departments. Cumberland's Billy Holding was the last line of defence in the first round at Barrow in February and kicked four goals in a 17-8 victory, but suffered a broken leg in a league game at Leeds a week later.

The injury was a double blow to Holding. Not only did it cost him a place at Wembley, it also ruled him out of contention for the Great Britain tour to Australia and New Zealand at the end of the season. Holding had already played in the first tour trial at Salford and earned positive reviews.

'Observer' in the *Daily Dispatch* had reported: "Holding gave a very sound display in every respect. Not quite so polished as Sullivan, but equally accurate in catching and kicking. Holding deserves another trial and must be considered in the running." Meanwhile 'Centre' in the *News Chronicle* had decided: "Holding fulfilled the highest expectations."

Local lad Harold Palin took over the full-back role for the second round tie at Halifax. It was the 19-year-old's first-team debut for Warrington and, in front of a passionate 19,000-strong crowd at Thrum Hall, it was a real baptism of fire. Palin, however, did well, even though Warrington trailed 2-0 for much of the match until Shankland kicked an equalising penalty goal in the last few minutes.

Palin kept his place in the team for the replay at Wilderspool the following Thursday afternoon. The tie attracted another large crowd, this time 16,749

THE R.L. CUP SEMI-FINAL AT WIGAN.—BY BERT WRIGHT. WARRINGTON BEAT Salford by seven points to two.

Liverpool Evening Express cartoonist Bert Wright pays tribute to Warrington's unexpected 7-2 victory over Salford in the 1936 Challenge Cup semi-final.

Warrington five days before the Wembley Final. Left to right, standing: Councillor J Canon Bardsley (chairman), Dave Cotton, Norman Rutledge, Sam Hardman, Billy Holding, Jack Chadwick, Jack Arkwright, Bill Chapman, Mick Flannery, Billy Dingsdale, Billy Bennett (trainer). Seated: Jack Goodall, Griff Jenkins, Bill Shankland (captain), Ben Hawker, Jack Miller. Front: Jack Garrett & Jim Newcomb.

mainly Warrington supporters, who were rewarded with an 18-15 victory. Centre Bill Shankland was again the key man for Warrington with a try and five goals.

New Zealander Roy Hazelhurst was the full-back for the third-round tie against Wigan at Wilderspool, a match that attracted a record crowd of almost 29,000. Hazelhurst was back after injury as was Billy Dingsdale, the former Warrington captain and Great Britain centre.

Dingsdale marshalled the backs superbly, the forwards were outstanding and Warrington won 5-2 with scrum-half Jack Goodall scoring the only try of the afternoon and second-row forward Mick Flannery kicking his first goal for the club.

Warrington were paired with their bogey team, Salford, who had already beaten them three times that season, in the semi-final at Wigan in March. Full-back Billy Holding, captain Bill Shankland and winger Griff Jenkins were all injured and Warrington were given little chance of success.

Still, supporters turned up at Central Park in record numbers with 41,538 paying ground record receipts of £2,704/7/4. Among the Warrington contingent was a mascot by the name of 'Nobbler' Burton who pushed a pram around the ground before the kick-off. The pram held a doll with a model of the cup.

Bill Baxter was the Warrington full-back on this occasion and his team struck first with scrum-half Jack Goodall crossing for a try after 12 minutes. Mick Flannery again added the goal but the key passage of play came in the moments leading up to half-time.

Warrington were hammering away at the Salford line and forced a drop out which was taken by centre Gus Risman. Second-row forward Jack Arkwright caught the ball, steadied himself and kicked a brilliant drop goal to make the half-time score 7-0 and give Warrington some valuable breathing space.

Gus Risman kicked a penalty goal after 50 minutes to close the gap to five points but Warrington were not to be denied. The Warrington forwards had again been outstanding and were hailed as "The Terrible Six" for their heroic efforts.

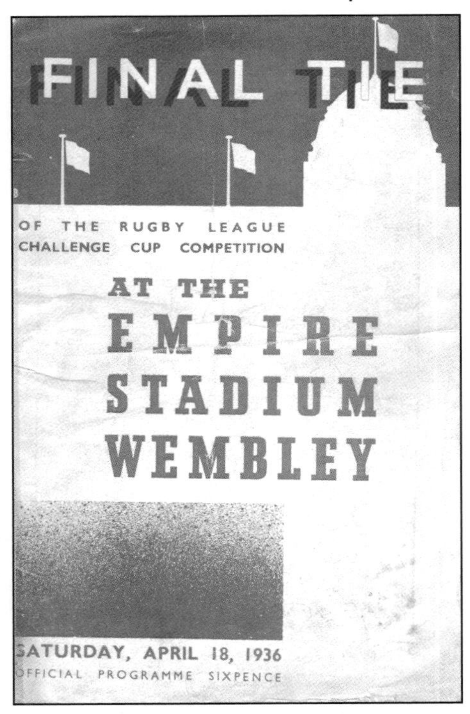

The front cover of the 1936 Challenge Cup Final programme.
(Courtesy RFL, programme supplied by Alan Domville)

In the build-up to the Final in April, Bill Shankland, by now the professional at Haydock Park Golf Club, and winger Griff Jenkins returned from injury, leaving Billy Holding as the only long-term casualty. "We are ready," declared Shankland before Warrington set off to their Hendon hotel on the eve of the Final.

Fifteen special trains were chartered to take supporters to London – the return fare was 15/6d – but the day was again destined to end in disappointment.

1936 Challenge Cup Final
Warrington versus Leeds at Wembley Stadium, 18 April 1936.
Attendance: 51,250.

Warrington had lost the 1928 Challenge Cup Final by two points (5-3) and the 1933 Challenge Cup Final by four points (21-17) so the very least Warrington fans expected as they travelled to Wembley was a close contest.

It was not to be. Warrington were well beaten by Leeds, 18-2, and would probably have suffered an even bigger defeat had hooker Dave Cotton not heeled the ball from 70 per cent of the scrums. Cotton took the first-half scrum battle 22-8 and the second-half 24-16, meaning he had won the ball from 46 of the game's 70 scrummages.

Bill Shankland, playing at full-back and again captaining the side, was drawn into numerous kicking duels with his opposite number Jim Brough, which the Leeds man dominated.

Some of the Warrington supporters who arrived in London early on the big day went to see the town's new MP, the Conservative barrister Mr Noel B. Goldie KC, and were given a tour of the House of Commons.

When the game kicked off, Warrington were given a lesson in rugby as Leeds won comfortably by four tries to nil, with scrum-half Evan Williams adding three goals.

Loose-forward Iowerth Isaac scored the opening try after eight minutes, although he was clearly offside when Leeds's Australian winger Eric Harris kicked ahead. Williams added the goal before Shankland kicked a penalty to make the score 5-2 after half an hour.

A try from centre Fred Harris after 33 minutes and a Williams penalty goal shortly before half-time made the score 10-2 at the interval. Eric Harris, who was known as the 'Toowoomba Ghost' because he was so difficult to catch, ended the match as a contest with Leeds's third try after 66 minutes.

He surged infield to leave three defenders standing, kicked ahead, regained possession and burst through two forlorn tacklers to score his 56th try of the season, which put the result beyond doubt. Williams added the goal to make it 15-2. Centre Gwyn Parker completed the rout five minutes from the end.

"No one was more disappointed at our failure than the players themselves, and you can hardly imagine our feelings," said Shankland. "We were beaten by a better side. We just did not strike our best form. There is no doubt we did our best, but our best was not good enough."

At least the final produced a record attendance – 51,250 – and record receipts – £7,070 – for any rugby league game in England as the competition continued to grow in stature.

Warrington: W.J. Shankland, J.W. Garrett, A.B. Hawker, W. Dingsdale, G. Jenkins, J. Newcombe, P.J. Goodall, J. Miller, D. Cotton, S. Hardman, M. Flannery, J. Arkwright, J. Chadwick.

Leeds: J.W. Brough, E. Harris, F. Harris, G. Parker, S. Brogden, A.R. Ralph, E. Williams, S.J. Satterthwaite, J. Hall, D. Dyer, K. Jubb, J. A. Casewell, I. Isaac.

Referee: A.S. Dobson (Featherstone).

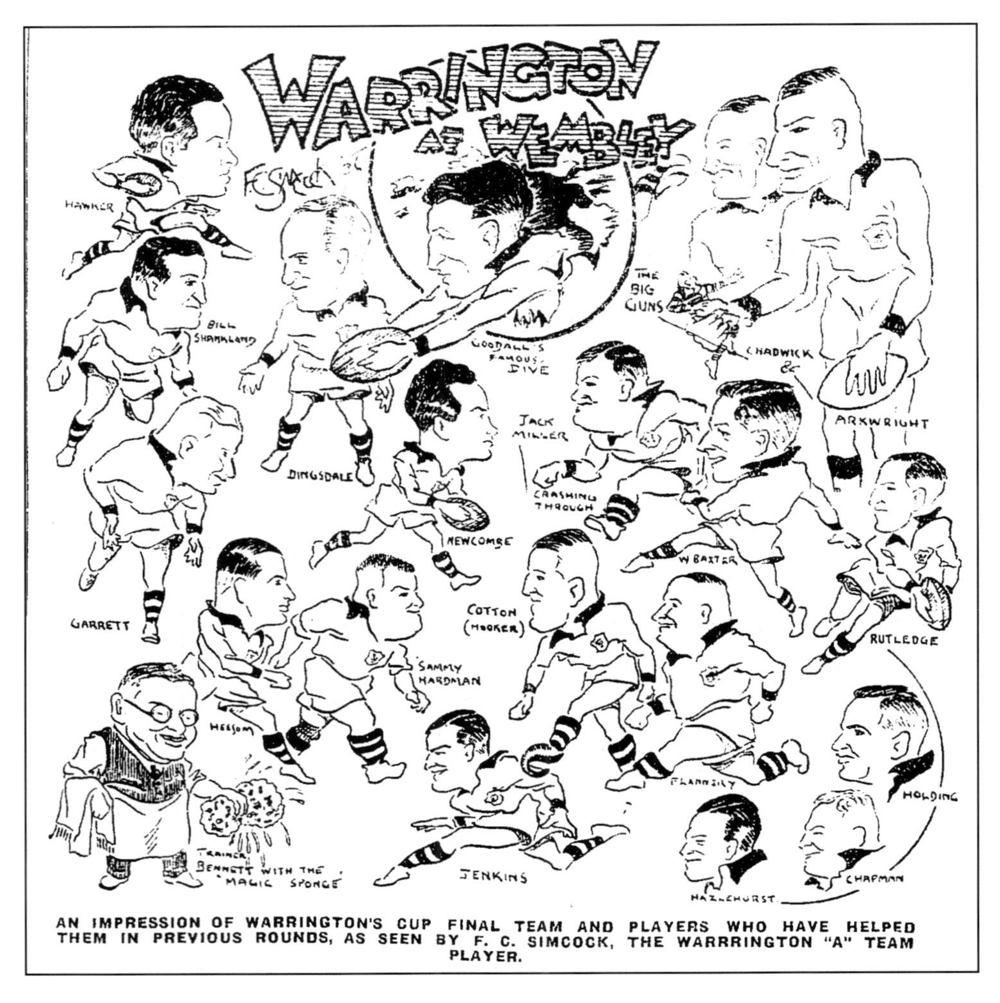

AN IMPRESSION OF WARRINGTON'S CUP FINAL TEAM AND PLAYERS WHO HAVE HELPED THEM IN PREVIOUS ROUNDS, AS SEEN BY F. C. SIMCOCK, THE WARRRINGTON "A" TEAM PLAYER.

'A' team regular Fred Simcock showed he was a man of many talents by drawing Warrington's Wembley squad for the *Warrington Examiner*.
Note trainer Billy Bennett with his magic sponge.

Warrington winger Griff Jenkins tries to tackle Eric Harris of Leeds during the 1936 Challenge Cup Final at Wembley.

Daily Dispatch cartoonist Gannon wondered if Yorkshire could complete a Challenge Cup and FA Cup double after Leeds had thrashed Warrington 18-2. It was not to be as Sheffield United lost the FA Cup Final 1-0 to Arsenal seven days later.

Two of Warrington's Wembley forwards – Jack Arkwright and Jack 'Cod' Miller – had the considerable consolation of a Great Britain tour to look forward to, along with club secretary Bob Anderton who had again been appointed joint manager. Anderton even missed the Challenge Cup Final because he was on the SS Cathay in the Bay of Biscay with the tour party and had to settle for radio commentary by the noted broadcaster Lance Todd. Arkwright and Miller joined the ship at Marseilles, having travelled overland.

For Miller, going on the tour was a fitting reward for 10 years of dedication and application following his Warrington debut as a chubby-faced youngster in December 1926. By the summer of 1936, he had already made 350 appearances and his career still had 10 years to run. He had earned his nickname 'Cod' by selling fresh fish from door-to-door. He earned his reputation as a great prop-forward by sheer willpower.

Arkwright, meanwhile, made unusual sporting history during the tour when he was sent off twice in the same match. The bizarre goings-on happened when the tourists were playing Northern Districts, one of the tough provincial teams.

Years later Arkwright recalled: "I tackled one of their players a bit hard and another bloke burst up and jumped on me. I thumped him and the referee ordered me off; but their captain, possibly with revenge in mind, made a plea on my behalf. The referee relented.

"After taking more stick and with only two minutes of the match remaining I thumped their captain. The referee spotted me. 'All right,' I said. 'I'm going this time.' And I walked."

Three days later Arkwright was sent off again, after laying out the Australian prop-forward Ray Stehr in the third test between the Kangaroos and Great Britain at the Sydney Cricket Ground. Famously, the brass band played *Goodnight Sweetheart* as he left the field. When, eventually, he was revived, Stehr was sent off too. Arkwright was 6 feet 3 inches and 16 stones and not a person with whom one would take liberties.

If Arkwright was the biggest player at the club then 19-year-old scrum-half Frank Cueto, who was signed from Maryport in Cumberland in March, was the smallest. Cueto, who had played two trial games for the 'A' team under the name of Kimberley, was of Spanish parentage, but English birth and, incredibly, weighed just nine stones. Cueto had received a £200 signing-on fee and, one imagines, instructions to beef himself up.

A Wilderspool hero: Jack Miller

Prop-forward Jack 'Cod' Miller was Warrington's steamroller: big, strong, powerful and relentless. Between the wars he made more first-team appearances than any other Warrington player, a whopping 470. He also went on the 1936 Great Britain tour of Australia and New Zealand, won four England caps and played three times for Lancashire.

Jack Arkwright and Jack Miller on board the SS Cathay.

Born and bred in Leigh, Miller made his Warrington debut at St Helens in December 1926 at the age of 20. His career was soon to be interrupted, however, by one of the most bizarre injuries ever suffered by a Warrington player: Miller fractured a forearm while starting up a car with a starting handle.

He was back in the front row the following season though and that is where he stayed, through good times and bad, until his final appearance in February 1946, aged 39, after which he signed for Leigh. Even his wedding day did not curtail his Warrington career. He simply got married in the morning and turned out at Wilderspool in the afternoon.

Miller was a member of three Lancashire Cup-winning teams, in 1929, 1932 and 1937; and three Challenge Cup Final losing teams, in 1928, 1933 and 1936.

In his pomp, he was 5 feet 8 inches and weighed 14 stones 6 pounds, although in the early 1930s he seemed to be piling on the pounds until a programme of strict training gave him a physique to be proud of and made him one of the fittest men in the team.

All that hard work paid off with a place on the 1936 Lions tour and with appearances in two Championship Finals, against Swinton in 1935 and against Salford in 1937. He even collected a Challenge Cup winners' medal, at the fourth attempt, as a guest player with Huddersfield in 1945.

Miller died, aged 72, in October 1978 and was elected to the club's Hall of Fame as a founder member in 2003.

18. 1936-37: The Don Bradman of rugby league

Club president: Joe Tilling. Club captain: Jack Arkwright.

Once again, Warrington rang the changes in their hunger for success, appointing Chris Brockbank, the former Swinton, Salford and Bradford Northern winger, as their first team manager. The days when the committee picked the team were coming to an end.

Brockbank had been the coach of Huddersfield on their visits to Wembley in 1933 and 1935 but was coaching Bradford Park Avenue football team when Warrington lured him back to rugby league in the summer of 1936.

His arrival and new training methods produced a remarkable improvement in Warrington's home form. They won 17 and drew one of their 18 league games at Wilderspool and were awarded two points for the match against the London club Streatham and Mitcham, which was not played after their opponents withdrew from the competition.

As well as a new manager, Warrington also had a new captain, Jack Arkwright, and a new vice-captain, Billy Holding, happily recovered from his broken leg. There were two new signings from Wales, too. Nineteen-year-old stand-off Mel de Lloyd, from Llanelli RUFC, was the first to arrive, in September. De Lloyd, who was just 5 feet 7 inches tall, was tempted north by a signing-on fee of £300 and was plunged straight into the first team. He responded by making an impressive debut as Oldham were beaten 15-7 at Wilderspool in front of 10,000 fans.

Les Jones, aged 20, the brilliant Penycraig and Glamorgan rugby union full-back, followed in October. Jones, who was 5 feet 10 inches tall and weighed 11 stones 2 pounds, received a £350 signing-on fee. He, too, was soon handed his first-team debut, against Barrow at Wilderspool on Saturday 31 October. Billy Holding was absent on county duty with Cumberland and so Jones was promoted from the 'A' team. He thought he had marked the occasion with a long-range drop goal but the referee ruled that the ball had dipped under the crossbar at the last second. Fortunately, Warrington still won 9-8.

Away from rugby league, this was the day when the 207 Jarrow Marchers arrived in London after their 280 mile trek to protest about unemployment and poverty in the North East. Stanley Baldwin, the Prime Minister of the day, infamously refused to see any of their representatives.

The arrival of Jones meant there was no room for local full-back Harold Palin, who was transferred to Swinton. Palin, of course, would return to Wilderspool as a mighty second-row forward 11 years later.

Another full-back from the 1936 Challenge Cup run, the New Zealander Roy Hazelhust, was transferred to the Roanne club in France where he was appointed trainer-coach.

Warrington made an even more sensational signing, that of centre Dave Brown, the Australian captain, in November 1936. Brown had been christened "the Don Bradman of rugby league" in Sydney because of his phenomenal points-scoring ability. Remarkably, it was Brown, aged 23, who first approached Warrington when he posted an airmail letter to Wilderspool from Sydney on 10 October. The Warrington committee could not believe their luck.

To complete the signing, on a four-year contract, Warrington agreed to part with record sums of money – £500 up front with another £500 to follow during the rest of the season with five per cent interest added, and £6 per match, win, lose or draw. Warrington also had to pay a £200 transfer fee to the Australian rugby league as compensation for them losing one of their brightest stars.

Brown and his new wife set sail from Australia on 1 December. They arrived in Southampton on 11 January, where they were met by club secretary Bob Anderton, and reached Warrington the following day. A large crowd, including Bill Shankland, were gathered on the platform at Bank Quay Station to greet them. The Browns then went to stay with the Shanklands at their home in Grappenhall.

Brown, who weighed 12 stones 6 pounds, made his debut for Warrington 'A' against Wigan 'A' in the Lancashire Senior Competition at Wilderspool on Saturday 16 January. Brown's appearance attracted a crowd of 10,000, a record for a reserve team fixture. Warrington lost 17-11, but not before Brown had scored a try near the end.

He made his first-team debut seven days later, against Leigh at Wilderspool, and again scored a try in a 41-2 victory. Brown was given a standing ovation as he ran out on to the field, as was Tommy Thompson, the Leigh captain and former Warrington winger. Warrington's current wingers had a field day with Griff Jenkins scoring three tries and Jack Garrett one. Full-back Billy Holding kicked seven goals.

Brown's next appearance was again at Wilderspool, against the league leaders Salford, and again he scored a try as Warrington won 11-0 in front of 16,000 delighted fans. He went on to make 93 appearances for Warrington, scoring 48 tries and kicking 91 goals, but he never quite came to terms with the cold English winters.

His fifth match for Warrington, at Bradford Northern on 20 February, should have given him a clue of what to expect. The game was abandoned after 34 minutes, with Warrington losing 4-0, because of a snowstorm. When the players had left the field, however, the sun came out and some spectators protested because the game was not restarted. The referee intervened and said that the pitch was unfit and that both captains had appealed for the game to be stopped.

Warrington's next league game was at home to Wakefield on 6 March when both teams were followed out on to the pitch by flyweight boxer Peter Kane from Golborne, fresh from a lightning quick victory in Paris the previous Monday. Kane was given a huge cheer by the 16,000 crowd.

The Bradford match was rearranged for Wednesday 7 April, but again had to be postponed following a thunderstorm. It was finally played the following Monday with Warrington winning 14-2. Brown kicked a goal.

That victory set the stage perfectly for Warrington's next home game, against Liverpool Stanley. If Warrington won they would qualify for the top four Championship play-offs. A crowd of 20,000 turned out to cheer them on and were rewarded with a 16-11 victory featuring two Bill Shankland tries and two Dave Brown goals.

The Wire went on to clinch second place in the table with 59 points - equalling the record tally set two years earlier - and earn a Championship semi-final against Leeds at Wilderspool.

Northern Rugby League – top of the table

	P	W	D	L	F	A	Pts
Salford	38	29	3	6	529	196	61
Warrington	38	28	3	7	468	189	59
Leeds	38	28	1	9	627	262	57
Liverpool Stanley	38	26	3	9	425	226	55

Brown, as well as having a deceptive change of pace and an eye for an opening, was also a fearless tackler and a gutsy competitor, qualities that almost proved costly in the semi-final when he was concussed in the opening minutes of the match.

By the final 15 minutes of the game it became clear that he was not in full command of his senses and, in the dressing room afterwards, the only thing he could remember was shaking hands with one of the Leeds players before the kick-off. He could not even remember the goalkick he attempted from near the touchline in the second half as Warrington inched towards a 12-2 victory in front of a 22,000-strong crowd thanks to two late tries from veteran centre Billy Dingsdale.

Full-back Billy Holding, besides playing one of the best games of his career, kicked three fine goals. The first, after 30 seconds, was a penalty goal from two yards in from touch and almost on the halfway line. Brown, of course, could not remember anything about that and the final, too, proved to be a game to forget.

1937 Championship Final

Warrington versus Salford at Central Park, Wigan, 1 May 1937.
Attendance: 31,500.

This was Warrington's third Championship Final but any hopes that it would prove to be a case of third time lucky were cruelly denied.

Warrington centre Dave Brown and full-back Billy Holding were both injured in the opening quarter of the match but – because substitutes were not allowed – they had to continue playing.

The Warrington squad and officials for the 1937 Championship Final. Left to right, back: Stan Jones (treasurer), Joe Tilling (president), Dave Cotton, G. Hollingworth, Les Jones, Frank Cueto, Dave Brown, Bill Rankin, Eric Welsby, P.F. Ward (chairman), Chris Brockbank (manager). Middle: Bob Anderton (secretary), Bill Shankland, Bill Chapman, Billy Holding, Jack Arkwright (captain), Billy Dingsdale, Griff Jenkins. Front: Jack Miller, Mel de Lloyd and Jack Goodall. (Courtesy Stan Lewandowski)

Both men suffered groin strains when tackling Emlyn Jenkins, the Salford stand-off, and both were sent to hobble on the right wing with Bill Chapman switched from loose-forward to right centre to keep them company. Bill Shankland was moved from right wing to full-back.

Warrington were now horribly unbalanced and disjointed but, with seven minutes remaining, still led 11-8. It was, however, too good to last. Salford scored a try in the corner through winger Barney Hudson and Gus Risman, the Great Britain centre, kicked a magnificent goal from the touchline to give them a 13-11 victory. Warrington did not deserve to lose and with 13 fit men would undoubtedly have won.

Still, Warrington should have made a dream start to the Final because, with less than two minutes on the clock, centre Billy Dingsdale passed to Dave Brown in a wonderful position. Brown was 10 yards from the Salford line with Bill Shankland in support and just one man to beat. Inexplicably, Brown dropped the pass. Warrington quickly put that blunder behind them and two penalty goals from Billy Holding, after eight minutes and 15 minutes, gave them a 4-0 lead before Gus Risman replied with two penalties of his own to level the scores.

Following Holding's injury, Shankland took over the goalkicking duties and kicked another penalty five minutes before half-time to put Warrington 6-4 ahead at the break. A drop goal from second-row forward Eric Welsby, the only one of his career, then stretched the lead to 8-4 as the tension mounted.

Two more Gus Risman penalty goals, after 55 minutes and 60 minutes, again levelled the scores before a great run by prop Jack 'Cod' Miller created a rare try for hooker Dave Cotton. Crucially, Shankland missed the kick but Warrington were still three points ahead and starting to think the unthinkable.

It was not to be and after losing two Challenge Cup Finals and now two Championship Finals in the space of five seasons it seemed that Warrington were destined to never again lift one of the game's major prizes.

Warrington: W.J. Holding, W.J. Shankland, D. Brown, W. Dingsdale, G. Jenkins, M. De Lloyd, P.J. Goodall, W. Rankin, D. Cotton, J. Miller, J. Arkwright, E. Welsby, W. Chapman.
Salford: H. Osbaldestin, B. Hudson, A. Gear, A.J. Risman, A. Edwards, E. Jenkins, W. Watkins, H.A. Williams, H.C. Day, J. Bradbury, P. Dalton, B. Cambridge, J. Feetham.
Referee: F Peel (Bradford).

Warrington's season did not end with the Final because they had accepted invitations to play in two sevens tournaments. At Belle Vue on Wednesday 12 May, the team reached the final, beating Wigan 13-0 in the first round and Widnes 5-0 in the semi-final. The final itself went to extra time before Warrington lost 7-2 to Oldham. A Mel de Lloyd penalty goal had given Warrington the lead in the second half of normal time.

Warrington's season finished at Headingley on 15 May when they lost 11-3 to Hunslet, the eventual winners, in the first round of the traditional end-of-season Leeds Sevens which attracted a crowd of 10,000. The Warrington team for both tournaments was De Lloyd, Griff Jenkins, Les Jones, Frank Cueto, Eric Welsby, John Rothwell, and G. Hollingsworth.

Warrington had only suffered one home defeat during the season, 7-6 against Wigan in the first round of the Lancashire Cup, but it meant Wilderspool again staged the Final between Salford and Wigan that attracted a crowd of 17,500 despite bad weather.

Wilderspool also staged the Challenge Cup semi-final between Widnes and Wigan. Widnes won 13-9 in front of a 29,000 crowd and went on to lift the cup by beating Keighley in the Final at Wembley.

Disappointingly, Warrington had gone out in the third round at Wakefield after pulling off a stunning 10-4 win at Salford in the first round. That match attracted a record crowd of 26,470 to the Willows – one that still stands.

Clarrie Owen, who would later become a Warrington director, attended the match as a 14-year-old schoolboy: "Salford were one of the best teams in the country and we were given no chance of winning," he recalled. "It was bitterly cold, the pitch was muddy and the ball was heavy. When the Salford scrum-half fed the ball at a scrum, he deliberately threw it into the face of Dave Cotton, the Warrington hooker. Suddenly, Cotton's fist emerged from the scrum and flattened him. He was out cold for a couple of minutes. Cotton and second-row forward Jack Arkwright, the Warrington captain at the time, were hard men, playing a tough game in difficult conditions."

Scrum-half Jack Goodall scored the only try in the 5-4 second round victory at York, diving over from a scrum close to the try line. Full-back Billy Holding missed the Wakefield game with flu and so young Les Jones took his place and played brilliantly. Yet Warrington sorely missed Holding's goalkicking prowess as they could easily have won the tie on penalty goals alone.

In the second half of the season, Warrington made two more major signings. In March, following the Challenge Cup defeat at Wakefield, they signed the winger Islwyn 'Izzy' Davies from St Helens. Davies made his debut at Leigh later the same day and celebrated with a hat-trick of tries. Two weeks later he went one better by scoring four tries against Swinton.

At the end of April, Warrington announced that they had signed the Welsh rugby union international forward Ivor Bennett of Aberavon. Bennett, aged 22, had played nine times for Glamorgan and represented Wales against Ireland in Belfast that season. Weighing 14 stones 6 pounds and standing at 6 feet 1 inch, he could play anywhere in the pack. Bennett received a £400 signing-on fee with another £100 to follow after he had completed six first-team matches. But it wasn't all good news. Despite reaching the Championship Final, Warrington's spending spree on players meant they recorded a hefty loss of £1,664 over the season.

It had been another extraordinary campaign but perhaps not quite as extraordinary as the match between Wigan 'A' and Liverpool Stanley 'A' at Central Park in March when eight players were sent off, four from each side, and two were carried off injured. The eight dismissed players were banned for four matches each.

On a brighter note, Ben Hawker, Warrington's Welsh centre, was selected for the two-week Northern Rugby League tour of France in January and February and played in all four matches, scoring four tries.

Among the past players who died during the season was James Holmes, aged 70, who had been a forward in the late 1880s and early 1890s. In his youth, Holmes had been a well-known athlete, winning many prizes on the running track and specialising in 300-yard races. In 1888, he was also a member of Warrington's champion gymnastics team.

Like many former rugby players, he became a pub landlord and, from 1917 to his retirement in 1935, he was the licensee of the Vulcan Hotel on Dallam Lane. He died at home at Long Lane, Orford in May 1937.

A Wilderspool hero: Jack Arkwright

Rugby league is, and probably always has been, a young man's game but there have always been exceptions to the rule. Big Jack Arkwright, for example, played his final game for Warrington at Hunslet in September 1945, at the age of 42, creating a club record that will almost certainly never be broken.

His best days, however, were from September 1934, when he was signed from St Helens for a then club record £700, a massive sum at the time, to the outbreak of the Second World War five years later.

During that time he made more than 150 appearances for Warrington, at the rate of 31 per season, and represented Lancashire eight times, England four times and Great Britain six times.

Arkwright was a big man, even for a second-row forward, and physical intimidation was part of his armoury. He certainly made a big impression on Dai Davies, the former Warrington scrum-half, after the latter had joined Huddersfield and found himself face-to-face with him on the field: "I came up against this ugly-looking forward playing with Warrington called Arkwright," recalled Davies. "He was a new recruit and he was one of the dirtiest players I ever saw. He'd be out to maim you, hurt you. I had a few words with him on the field and he hit me across the face with a backhander."

Arkwright was not quite the unthinking brute that Davies described. In 1935 he persuaded the Warrington committee to sign Dave Cotton, the St Helens hooker, and he went on to become one of the best number nines in the club's history.

The following year, he was appointed club captain and led Warrington to their 1937 Lancashire Cup Final victory over Barrow, setting up the first of Dave Brown's two tries with a clever kick.

But he was not immune from the 'So close to glory' curse and played in three finals in three years with Warrington – the 1935 Championship Final, the 1936 Challenge Cup Final and the 1937 Championship Final – all of which were lost.

Arkwright's son, Jack, and grandson, Chris, followed him into professional rugby league without quite reaching his dizzy heights. Arkwright died, aged 87, in January 1990 and was one of the first players to be inducted into the club's Hall of Fame when it was established in January 2003. He was already a founder member of the St Helens Hall of Fame.

Incredibly, Arkwright had only started playing rugby league because the factory where he worked told him that he had to play football for them and not a rival club. "It put me off," he said. "I liked making my own mind up, so I had a go with my local rugby league team, Sutton Commercial, who were known as the Comics."

Inevitably, he soon attracted the attention of several professional clubs: "A chap came from Batley with £50 in his hand. I said: 'where's Batley? I've never been out of Sutton!'"

Arkwright, though, was not a fan of the modern game: "It's just like tick rugby. It just gets on my nerves people not tackling properly."

Left: Dave Brown was one of the highest-paid players in the game in 1937, earning £6 per match – win, lose or draw. (Courtesy Warrington Museum). Right: Emlyn Jenkins helped Salford defeat Warrington in the 1937 Championship final before becoming the Warrington coach 10 years later.

Jack Arkwright (right), Warrington's captain from 1936 to 1939, shakes hands with Harry Beverley of Halifax before a match at Thrum Hall.

19. 1937-38: A world record signing

Club president: Joe Tilling. Club captain: Jack Arkwright.

Warrington began the season by apologising to their fans although, in truth, they had nothing to apologise about. The eccentricities of the fixture list which, of course, continue to this day, had left Warrington with three successive away games in September. So after opening the campaign against Oldham at Wilderspool on 28 August, their next home fixture was on 25 September, four weeks later. Warrington faced three successive away games again in March and April and so complained to the league management committee.

The committee admitted that Warrington had a real grievance but refused to make any changes to the fixture list and so the club put an apology in the programme. Despite that obvious irritation, Warrington won two trophies, completing a Lancashire Cup and Lancashire League double, although there was still an element of disappointment because they missed out on the Championship play-offs altogether by finishing fifth.

During the summer of 1937, Warrington's committee had shown that they, at least, were thinking on their feet by funding more ground improvements and another major signing. Another bay was added to the main stand, the work was carried out by Messrs Pearson & Knowles and Harry Fairclough, to take the number of seats up to 2,250. The major signing was the diminutive Dai Parker from Neath, who had been described as the best rugby union scrum-half in Wales the previous season when he was a reserve for the international matches. At 5 feet 3 inches tall and weighing just 9 stones, Parker was the smallest player in the league although, on the positive side, he had played junior rugby with Mel de Lloyd, Warrington's other Welsh half-back.

Warrington won their first eight matches – three at home and five away – as they made an excellent start to the league season and reached the Final of the Lancashire Cup.

A thrilling 80-yard try from Jack Garrett, the Warrington winger, on the hour mark was the highlight of the 12-5 win at Wigan in the league, a match that was played before a crowd of 25,000. Garrett, who was on the transfer list at the time, received a quick pass from Frank Cueto, the Warrington scrum-half, inside his own '25' and sidestepped two opponents. He then wriggled away from an attempted tackle and raced to the halfway line before kicking the ball over Jim Sullivan's head.

A desperate race between Garrett and two Wigan defenders followed which the Warrington man won with a sudden burst of acceleration. He then dribbled the ball over the line and touched down for a memorable score. He was taken off the transfer list soon after.

The Lancashire Cup Final, against Barrow at Central Park on Saturday, 23 October, was spoiled by terrible weather on the morning of the match making for a heavy pitch and reduced the attendance to just 14,000. Also on the morning of the match Warrington lost full-back Billy Holding to tonsillitis which meant that young Les 'Cowboy' Jones – aged just 21 – was called up for only his ninth first-team appearance.

Warrington's problems increased still further after only eight minutes when Jack Miller, who had been targeted by the Barrow pack, was sent off by Bradford referee Frank Peel for dissent. With captain Jack Arkwright to the fore, however, Warrington regrouped successfully and at half-time the score was still 0-0.

Early in the second half, Arkwright made ground and managed to send an angled kick towards the Barrow try line. In a flash, Dave Brown was on to it and touched down in the corner. Bill Shankland missed the conversion and Freddie French, the Barrow full-back, cut the lead to one point with a penalty goal. Shankland then burst through the Barrow defence and passed to stand-off Mel de Lloyd who sent Brown scampering over for his second try.

Shankland kicked the conversion and, although French kicked a second penalty goal to make the score 8-4, Warrington's 12 men held firm until the final whistle. Warrington fans invaded the pitch and Arkwright needed the help of several policemen to reach the main stand where he received the trophy from Lord Derby.

The club officials who attended the match, however, still had some important business to do. On their way back to Warrington they visited Liverpool to sign the Great Britain full-back Billy Belshaw from Liverpool Stanley for a world record fee of £1,450, plus a job for his father, something not made known at the time.

Belshaw, aged 24, was a brilliant attacking full-back and made his debut at home to Barrow a week later where he proved his all-round ability by producing a magnificent defensive effort and kicking five goals in a 28-7 victory. He also played in all three test matches against the touring Australians. For the first test, he was a Liverpool Stanley player, for the next two he was with Warrington. Great Britain appearances, incidentally, were now worth £10 a man – £7 win, lose or draw and £1 for each day in training.

Once again, the Kangaroos made two trips to Wilderspool, losing 7-5 to a Lancashire side including Warrington captain Jack Arkwright, who was being described as 'The Octopus' because of his formidable tackling technique, and then 8-6 to Warrington. In the club game, the Australians were accused of "vigorous and shady tactics" by the *Warrington Guardian* and had a forward, Gordon MacLennan sent off 15 minutes from time.

Warrington, however, were not to be denied and scrum-half Frank Cueto scored a brilliant try after 52 minutes to level the scores at 6-6. Picking the ball up from a scrum, the little half-back mesmerised three defenders, who were convinced he was going to pass to his centre Dave Brown, before diving over the line. Billy Belshaw missed the conversion but, five minutes later, Australia were penalised and Bill Shankland stepped up to condemn his fellow countrymen to an 8-6 defeat.

Despite the Kangaroos' dubious tactics, Warrington were still generous hosts and each tourist was presented with a number of souvenirs, including an ashtray from the club and a set of knives from the brewers Greenall Whitley. The match was followed by a benefit dance for Jack Miller and Sam Hardman, two veterans of the Warrington pack, at the Parr Hall.

In the middle of January, Warrington were on top of the league with 15 wins and a draw from their opening 19 matches, and Dave Brown was waxing lyrical in the *Evening Chronicle:* "Since I joined the Warrington club last January on a four-year contract I have been very happy," he said. "As a result of the publication of my signing-on terms I was afraid there might be a certain amount of aloofness by other players, but that was banished from my mind from the moment I arrived at Wilderspool. We are a really happy family and whatever success Warrington have achieved while I have been with them has not been due to one or two players, but to the magnificent team spirit which permeates the whole team. The same spirit prevails between players and officials and another important unit in our success is Chris Brockbank, our manager, who has a manner of his own of getting the best out of the boys under his care."

It was, of course, too good to last. Warrington's problems had begun against Rochdale Hornets at Wilderspool in December when winger Izzy Davies suffered a broken leg in the first minute of the game. Billy Belshaw then dislocated a shoulder while playing for Great Britain in the third test against Australia at Huddersfield.

Worse followed at Widnes on Christmas Day when Jack Arkwright and Mel de Lloyd were among four players sent off. Arkwright appealed against his dismissal, but was still banned for six matches. Warrington fans were not amused. If Arkwright was such a dirty player, they asked, why did the selectors keep picking him for Lancashire, England and Great Britain? De Lloyd was banned for three matches.

The problems grew and grew. Loose-forward Rex King returned home to New Zealand because of injury and Welsh second-row forward Ivor Bennett, who had taken to rugby league straight away, was sent off against Broughton Rangers and banned for two matches.

Warrington lost four games in a row, including the match against Hull at Wilderspool on Saturday 22 January, which had been set aside as a benefit day for Jack Miller and Sam Hardman who shared the gate receipts of £391.

The committee tried to stop the rot by signing the Cornish prop or second-row forward – and former all-in wrestler – Frank Gregory, aged 26, from Wigan. No sooner had he joined, however, than Ivor Bennett fractured a collarbone and Warrington were bundled out of the Challenge Cup in a first-round replay at home to Halifax.

Fortunately, Warrington still kept pulling out good results, if not great performances, against their fellow Lancashire clubs. St Helens Recs, for example, were beaten 12-5 at Wilderspool on a day when Warrington won the

Warrington captain Jack Arkwright prepares to receive the Lancashire Cup from Lord Derby while Bob Anderton holds a box containing the winners' medals.

Warrington's 1937 Lancashire Cup-winning team captained by the incomparable Jack Arkwright.

Cartoon time: How Gordon Roylance recorded Warrington's Lancashire Cup final victory over Barrow in the pages of the *Warrington Guardian*.

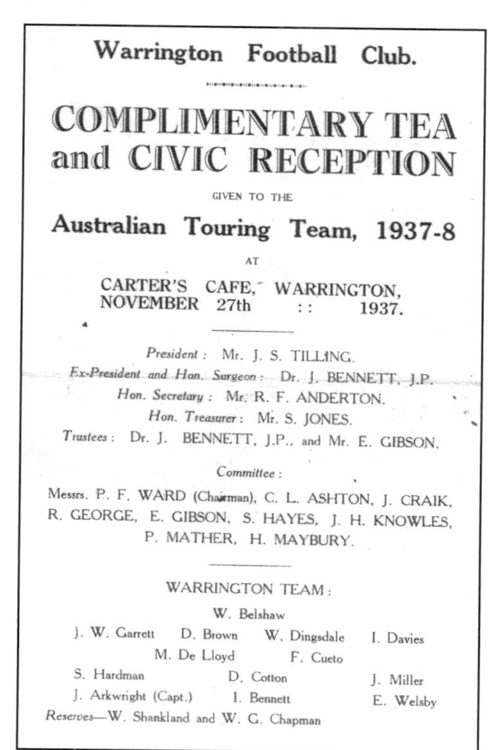

Warrington Football Club.

COMPLIMENTARY TEA and CIVIC RECEPTION

GIVEN TO THE

Australian Touring Team, 1937-8

AT

CARTER'S CAFE, WARRINGTON,
NOVEMBER 27th :: 1937.

President: Mr. J. S. TILLING.
Ex-President and Hon. Surgeon: Dr. J. BENNETT, J.P.
Hon. Secretary: Mr. R. F. ANDERTON.
Hon. Treasurer: Mr. S. JONES.
Trustees: Dr. J. BENNETT, J.P., and Mr. E. GIBSON.

Committee:

Messrs. P. F. WARD (Chairman), C. L. ASHTON, J. CRAIK, R. GEORGE, E. GIBSON, S. HAYES, J. H. KNOWLES, P. MATHER, H. MAYBURY.

WARRINGTON TEAM:

W. Belshaw
J. W. Garrett D. Brown W. Dingsdale I. Davies
M. De Lloyd F. Cueto
S. Hardman D. Cotton J. Miller
J. Arkwright (Capt.) I. Bennett E. Welsby
Reserves—W. Shankland and W. G. Chapman

Left: Warrington treated the 1937 Kangaroos to a complimentary tea and civic reception at Carter's Cafe in November.

Right: Les 'Cowboy' Jones played in the 1937 Lancashire Cup Final victory.

scrum battle 59-19 but failed to make the most of their huge amount of possession. Next, the Wire won at Leigh 14-2 on an afternoon when the Warrington committee members and players paid for their admission to help out the home club in a time of financial need.

Three more defeats followed at the end of March and beginning of April, at Oldham, Barrow and Leeds. At Oldham, second-row forward G. Hollingsworth, standing in for the ill Jack Arkwright, was sent off in the first half and later banned for three matches. At Barrow, three players – Billy Belshaw, Dave Brown and Les Jones – were all injured.

Finally, two defeats in two days over Easter – at home to Widnes on Good Friday in front of a 20,000-strong crowd and at Wakefield Trinity on Easter Saturday – saw the Wire slip out of the top four. The Widnes game was Bill Shankland's last for the club after a fantastic career spanning almost seven years and yielding 231 appearances, 74 tries and 70 goals. He had also captained the team at Wembley in 1933 and 1936.

The Widnes game also saw hooker Dave Cotton sent off in the later stages following the intervention of a touch judge. He was subsequently suspended for four matches. As ever, the *Warrington Guardian* summed things up perfectly: "Never in the history of Warrington have so many misfortunes befell the old organisation, for what with injuries to players and suspension of men, the committee have had the most serious difficulties to contend with."

All was not lost, however, and on Saturday 23 April, Warrington sealed their first Lancashire League title with a 32-5 victory over Leigh at Wilderspool in their last match of the season. Warrington had to win to take the title and victory was never in doubt. Australian Dave Brown scored a try in each half and Bill Chapman, Les Jones, Billy Belshaw and Jack Arkwright also touched down. Billy Holding converted all six tries and kicked a penalty goal.

At the end of the match, the Lancashire League trophy and medals were presented to Arkwright and his men by the Mayor of Warrington, Alderman Harry Sinclair, and the team posed for photographs. The 32 points they had scored meant that Warrington had the best attack in the league, having scored 534 points compared to 530 by Leeds – they should really have qualified for the Championship play-offs.

Australian centre Dave Brown had been a tower of strength, playing in every game and scoring 20 tries and kicking 36 goals. Teenage winger Ossie Peake, who had been signed directly from Newton-le-Willows Grammar School, had led the way in the 'A' team with 17 tries and was rewarded with his first-team debut at Leeds on 2 April.

Warrington's season was no doubt discussed at length the night before, at London's Dorchester Hotel, where a dinner was being held to celebrate jockey Steve Donoghue's first season as a trainer. After all, he had registered primrose and blue hoops as his racing colours. He had also established a fund to benefit the needy in his hometown of which there were many – too many.

Left: Billy Belshaw, pictured here in Lancashire kit, joined Warrington for a world record fee of £1,450 – plus a job for his father. Right: Warrington signed the Cornish prop or second-row forward Frank Gregory from Wigan in February 1938.

The Wire had played 42 games, but the club was still run very much on a part-time basis and a proposal for a full-time secretary-manager was overwhelmingly defeated at the annual general meeting.

As well as signing players, of course, during the season players were sold to clear the decks and balance the books. Scrum-half Jack Goodall, back-row forward Jack Chadwick and centre Norman Rutledge were all transferred to Keighley. Full-back Bill Baxter and second-row forward Mick Flannery were returned to Leigh.

Saddest of all, home-grown prop-forward Bill Rankin, who was 6 feet tall and weighed 14 stones, was sold to Rochdale Hornets in October, having played in the heroic Championship Final defeat against Salford just five months earlier.

When Rankin died aged 88 in May 1998, his nephew Tom admitted: "He always talked about playing for Warrington with great pride. He was devastated when they sold him to Rochdale."

A local hero: Peter Kane

Peter Kane was the Ricky Hatton of his day, a world champion boxer with the common touch. But while Hatton is a world-class light-welterweight, Kane made his mark in the flyweight division.

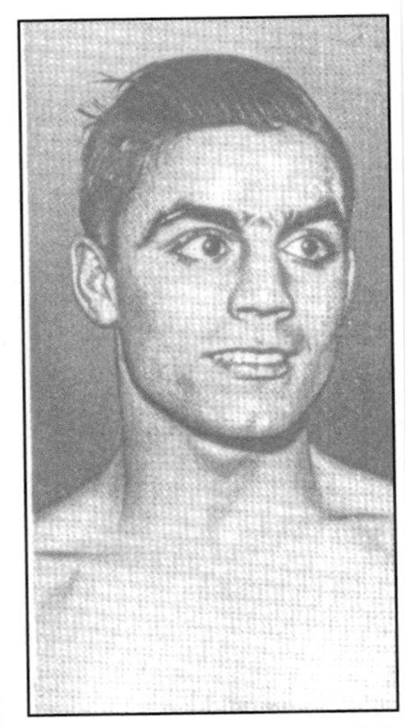

Born in Heywood, Lancashire in 1918, Kane grew up in Golborne after his family moved there before his first birthday and considered himself a Warringtonian. Throughout his boxing career, which ran to 102 professional bouts over 14 years, Kane worked for eight hours a day as a village blacksmith in Lowton. His day job gave him phenomenal upper body strength and a ferocious right hand and the inevitable nickname of 'The Golborne Blacksmith'.

After graduating from carnival boxing booths, Kane had his first professional fight in Liverpool. Before long, however, he was travelling to London to box and achieved a sequence of sensational victories over European fighters. He first fought for the world title, aged 19, in October 1937 when he took on the Scottish flyweight legend Benny Lynch in Glasgow in front of a lockout crowd of more than 40,000.

Kane made a dreadful start when he was knocked down in the first round but he got up and took the fight to the champion until he was felled twice more in the 12th round. By now, Kane was exhausted and his brave effort came to an end with two more knockdowns in the 13th.

Lynch surrendered the title in June 1938 when he failed to make the weight and Kane took the crown that September when he defeated the American Jackie Jurich in Liverpool. Two months later, Kane made his Wilderspool debut when he kicked off Billy Holding's testimonial match against Liverpool Stanley, an event that was recorded by the *Warrington Guardian's* resident cartoonist Gordon Roylance.

Kane was world champion from 1938 to 1943, although he was not an active boxer for much of that time because he was serving in the RAF. In total, he lost only seven of his 102 bouts and in 1994, three years after his death, he was rated as one of the top 10 fighters this country has ever produced in an article for the highly respected *The Ring* magazine.

20. 1938-39: A ray of sunshine

Club president: Joe Tilling. Club captain: Jack Arkwright.

In August 1938, Warrington and Wigan began a series of pre-season friendlies for the Wardonia Cup and, later, the Locker Cup that would continue for 57 years until the launch of Super League. It was decided that the proceeds of the matches would be divided equally between the clubs for distribution to local charities and junior rugby league. And, for the first match at least, each member of the winning team would receive a case of cutlery while each member of the losing side would be presented with a clock. The inaugural game, at Central Park, attracted a crowd of 8,000 and ended in a 17-17 draw before Jack Arkwright, the Warrington captain, won the cup on the toss of a coin. At last Warrington's luck was changing, but it was only a pre-season friendly and, much more importantly, Europe was lurching towards another war.

The following month, Neville Chamberlain, the British Prime Minister, returned from a meeting with Adolf Hitler in Munich to declare, wishfully, that he had secured "peace in our time". The reality was rather different and at half-time in the Lancashire Cup semi-final against Salford at Wilderspool on 29 September 1938, the club secretary, Bob Anderton, made an appeal through a loud speaker for fans to volunteer to act as air raid wardens. People were also being issued with gas masks.

But back in August, centre Dave Brown scored two tries and kicked three goals in that Wardonia Cup game and followed this with 18 tries in 30 appearances during the 1938-39 season. He also achieved a club record of sorts by scoring 51 points in the two league fixtures against Rochdale Hornets. At Rochdale on the opening day of the season, he scored four tries and kicked eight goals for a 28-point haul, while at Wilderspool on 5 November he scored a hat-trick of tries and kicked seven goals for a total of 23 points.

For once, however, the great Australian was overshadowed as Welsh winger Izzy Davies raced in for 34 tries, to eclipse the club record of 33 established by another Welsh winger, Steve Ray, six years earlier. Davies also scored two tries in two appearances for the English Rugby League team in France in November, taking his tally for the season to 36 and putting him second in the leading try scorers' list.

What made Davies's efforts all the more remarkable was the fact that he missed the opening nine games of the season after failing to agree a new contract. He did not make his first appearance until a 12-8 defeat at Castleford on Saturday 1 October when, inevitably, he scored a try. Davies quickly developed a particular liking for playing against Leigh, scoring 10 tries in three games against them, including five in the 30-0 victory at Wilderspool in April.

The war, of course, would cut many players' careers in two - notably, in Warrington's case, that of winger Ossie Peake. The teenage tyro failed to score in his first 10 games for the Wire but showed enough potential to earn a call-up to the Lancashire team playing Cumberland at Wigan on Wednesday 14 September. Peake marked the occasion with two tries, one a magnificent effort in which he ran half the length of the field, as Lancashire won 8-7.

Warrington had five players on county duty – Peake, Billy Belshaw and Jack Arkwright for Lancashire; Billy Holding and Frank Cueto for Cumberland – and all five had to play for the Wire the following night, at home to Wakefield. Not surprisingly, Warrington lost 21-10.

Peake finally got off the mark for Warrington with two brilliant tries in a 27-11 defeat at Halifax in his 11th appearance for the club and was already being tipped for international honours. Those calls would reach a crescendo on Saturday 24 September, when Peake raced in for four tries, two in each half, as Wigan were thrashed 36-8 at Wilderspool in front of 14,000 disbelieving fans. No other Warrington player, before or since, has enjoyed such a profitable afternoon against the cherry and whites.

Just as Peake's season was taking off, full-back Billy Holding was reaching the end of his Warrington career. His last match was the 14-8 victory over Liverpool Stanley at Wilderspool on Saturday 3 December when, in truth, he was only selected because it was his benefit match.

Holding, aged 31, was now the third-choice full-back behind Billy Belshaw and Les Jones but regularly, and uncomplainingly, turned out for the 'A' team. In fact, while playing for the 'A' team against Broughton Rangers 'A' at Wilderspool in October, he established another club record when he kicked 13 goals, from 15 attempts, in a 68-3 victory. By the time of his benefit match he had kicked more than 1,000 goals for the club, 833 for the first team and 188 for the reserves.

Warrington pulled out all the stops for the benefit match and that, of course, included recruiting a celebrity to perform the kick-off. They chose Golborne's Peter Kane, the world flyweight boxing champion. He had recently had an injured little finger amputated but was already thinking about his next fight.

Holding marked the occasion with his 834th and final goal for the first team. He had made 327 appearances over the course of 12 memorable seasons. There is, of course, little room for sentiment in professional sport and Holding was put on the transfer list at the end of January with a £200 price tag. He was later transferred to Rochdale Hornets but his goalkicking record at Warrington would stand until 1982, when it was bettered by Steve Hesford.

Scrum-half Dai Parker and centre Ben Hawker were also put on the list. Hawker had made 88 first-team appearances during a solid five-year career that had seen him score 30 tries and play in the 1935 Championship Final and 1936 Challenge Cup Final. Tragically, Hawker would hit the headlines again, in June 1951, when he murdered his wife Diana at their home in Nicholls Street, Grappenhall, before killing himself.

Despite the threat of war, Warrington were still planning for the future and in September, they signed a 19-year-old winger who played with the Pilkington's

Twelve of the Warrington team who played Castleford at Wilderspool on 14 January 1939. Left to right, standing: Frank Gregory, Dave Cotton, Alf Edge, Bill Chapman and Izzy Davies. Seated are Billy Dingsdale, Dave Brown, Jack Arkwright (captain), Jack Miller and Billy Belshaw. Front: Dai Parker and Mel de Lloyd. Missing is the loose-forward, Mason, who was about to make his debut. Perhaps he was still in the changing room with pre-match nerves. Warrington lost 27-13 after stand-off Mel de Lloyd was sent off.

Sheet Works team in St Helens and had also played some trials for the 'A' team under the pseudonym Pilkington. His real name was Albert Johnson and he was handed his first-team debut at home to Halifax on 21 January 1939. He weighed in at 11 stones 8 pounds, was 5 feet 9 inches tall and had an excellent sidestep. He would go on to join that select band of players to score more than 100 tries for the club.

Another local youngster, the 19-year-old Rylands Rec centre Fred Higginbottom, was signed in October after more successful trials with the 'A' team. Higginbottom, who was 5 feet 9 inches and weighed 11 stones 8 pounds, went on to make 90 first-team appearances between 1939 and 1947.

Another major signing arrived in January when Warrington snapped up the 22-year-old centre Gwynne Floyd from Maesteg. He was 5 feet 9 inches and 12 stone and had played county rugby union for Glamorgan. He was a very fast runner and had won numerous track events. He quickly settled in and scored two spectacular tries at Liverpool Stanley in April to seal a 12-4 victory.

During the season, Warrington achieved notable league doubles against Wigan, beating them 36-8 at home and 13-7 away, and Leeds, 17-7 at home and 8-5 away, but had to settle for seventh place in the final table.

Over the previous decade, club secretary Bob Anderton had given dozens of 'lantern talks' – slide shows – about the Great Britain tours to Australia and New Zealand in 1928, 1932 and 1936 to spread the rugby league gospel. He had addressed many schools and youth groups and even inmates at His Majesty's Prison in Liverpool. In March 1939, the prison chaplain, Hugh T. Smith, wrote to Anderton at the club to offer his thanks: "Your talk was excellent in every way – full of interest, of instruction, and of humour – whilst the pictures were a real joy," wrote the chaplain. "I thoroughly enjoyed every moment of the show and from the applause at the time and from subsequent remarks from individual men, there is no doubt about their verdict. All of us agree that it was a first-class performance.

"You may not always feel like a ray of sunshine, but you act like one here. To realise that you bring a bit of brightness into the drabness of prison life is perhaps sufficient reward to you for your generous service."

Also in March 1939, Ebenezer England, one of the seven founder members of the club, died in Warrington at the age of 81. His interest in the Wire had never faltered. He was a life member and regularly attended matches. The club had grown, matured and developed before his eyes. Wilderspool itself had been transformed from a field to a first-class sports stadium: "The playing pitch is a real picture and is in better condition than we have ever known it, whilst the new concrete terracing at the Wilderspool end has added considerably to making our ground a second Wembley," wrote Bob Anderton.

The Good Friday fixture at home to Salford illustrated the progress that had been made. It attracted a crowd of 22,000, including 5,000 from Salford, and featured a world-class display from Gus Risman, the Great Britain international, who scored all their points, three tries and two goals, to mastermind a 13-5 victory. However, two decades of strenuous efforts and moderate achievements from Warrington were drawing to a close.

At the end of the season, Dave Brown bought out the remaining 21 months of his contract and returned to Australia. Brown, who had just turned 26, had no grievance with the club, he was just homesick.

Also in May 1939, Warrington-born football winger Freddie Worrall, who had just been one of the stars of Portsmouth's 4-1 FA Cup Final triumph over Wolves, was one of the guests at the Warrington and District Football League's annual dinner and presentation evening at the Horse and Jockey Hotel on Winwick Road. After the war, of course, Worrall would join Warrington RLFC's coaching staff as a fitness trainer.

Bill Shankland, like Dai Davies before him, had left Warrington, without leaving his bad luck behind. By the summer of 1939, he was one of the world's leading professional golfers and, after three rounds of the Open Championship at St Andrews, he was lying second on 217 after rounds of 72, 73 and 72. A final round of 77, however, destroyed his chances and he finished four shots behind the winner, the Lancastrian Dick Burton, in a share of third place.

A local hero: Fred Worrall

To say that Warrington-born footballer Fred Worrall was superstitious barely does the word justice. Worrall was so concerned with having the fates on his side that for the 1939 FA Cup Final at Wembley, when he was playing on the right wing for Portsmouth, he had good luck charms tucked into each sock.

In the changing room before the match he also tied the laces of manager Jack Tinn's lucky spats, as he had done before every round on the road to Wembley. Still, all his efforts proved worthwhile as Portsmouth, the underdogs, beat the hot favourites, Wolverhampton Wanderers, 4-1 to give Worrall an FA Cup winners' medal to add to his two England caps.

Worrall, one of the most exciting wingers of his day, set up the fourth goal with a break down the right and a pinpoint cross that was duly headed home.

He was born in Warrington on 8 September 1910 and grew up in Hume Street. The slightly-built youngster began to prove himself a gifted footballer in the Oakwood Avenue School team. Spells with Witton Albion and Nantwich followed before, in December 1928, he joined Oldham Athletic where he scored 21 goals in 105 League appearances.

His big break came in October 1931 when he signed for First Division Portsmouth where he would score 65 goals in 309 League appearances. While at Fratton Park he also played in two FA Cup Finals - the first in 1934 resulted in a 2-1 defeat against Manchester City - and won his two England caps.

The first was against Holland in Amsterdam in May 1935 when he scored the only goal. The second came the following November at Stoke City's Victoria Ground and again he scored as England beat Northern Ireland 3-1.

Worrall played for Crewe Alexandra during the Second World War before finishing his career with a short spell at Stockport County. When his playing days were over he worked as a coach with Chester City and as a trainer and physiotherapist with Warrington RLFC when they were crowned champions for the first time in 1948 and won the Challenge Cup in 1950.

Football remained his first love, and in 1953, he was appointed the manager of Stockton Heath AFC, a post he held for 13 years. When he retired from Laporte Industries in 1975, after 17 years' service, former colleagues launched an annual works five-a-side competition for the Fred Worrall Challenge Trophy.

He died, aged 68, in Whiston Hospital on Good Friday 1979. His funeral was at St John's Church, Walton, and was attended by Roger Hunt, one of England's 1966 World Cup-winning team, who had played for him at Stockton Heath.

Warrington beat Wigan 14-11 in the Wardonia Cup at Wilderspool in August 1939, but the 1939-40 season was soon abandoned. Gordon Roylance captures the pre-season optimism in the *Warrington Guardian*.

Epilogue: The Wire at war 1939 to 1945

Warrington's first major signing in 1919 had been hooker Alf Peacock from Runcorn. Their last major signing in 1939 was also from a newly-disbanded club, the 22-year-old stand-off or centre Eli Dixon from St Helens Recs. Dixon, who was 5 feet 7 inches tall and weighed 11 stones 7 pounds, had been a reserve for Lancashire. Warrington also gave a trial to his brother Harry. Dixon's timing, however, was not as good as Peacock's because the 1939-40 season was only three games old when it was abandoned following the outbreak of the Second World War and supporters' and players' minds began to focus on more important events.

The third New Zealand touring team, under the captaincy of the former Warrington loose-forward Rex King, returned home following the outbreak of war – after just two games – to be with their families. King soon joined the war effort and later won the Military Cross for bravery on Crete, before he was captured there and spent the rest of the conflict as a prisoner.

The Rugby Football League decided to carry on under difficult circumstances and launched a War Emergency League in September 1939 with separate Lancashire and Yorkshire sections to cut down on travelling costs. Warrington played 22 games in the Lancashire Section in the 1939-40 season, winning 11, drawing one and losing 10. They also played two games in May – both against Wigan – in a short lived Lancashire Summer Competition, which had to be abandoned.

Warrington lost many players to the forces, but guest players from other clubs helped to plug the gaps. Old boys Jack Goodall and Jack Chadwick, both from Halifax, Billy Holding from Rochdale Hornets, and Vin Dilorenzo from Bradford Northern, all pulled on the primrose and blue of Warrington again.

One match at the start of the 1940-41 season brought the war right to Warrington's doorstep. While they were playing Broughton Rangers at Wilderspool on 14 September, a German aircraft attacked the Thames Board Mills factory at Arpley Meadows, less than a mile from the ground.

On 2 November, while Warrington were beating St Helens 13-0 at Knowsley Road, a friendly football international – of sorts – between England and Poland was staged at Wilderspool. It had been organised by officers of the United States Air Force based at Burtonwood and the match was kicked off by the Mayor of Warrington, Alderman William Roberts.

Warrington finished second to Wigan in the Lancashire League in 1940-41 with 13 victories and only three defeats from their 16 matches. Captain Billy Belshaw, stand-off or centre Eli Dixon and winger Ossie Peake led the way with 11 tries apiece – all of which are included in their official career records.

Wilderspool itself, however, was needed for the war effort – the ground was commandeered – and the main stand was used as a store room by the US Air

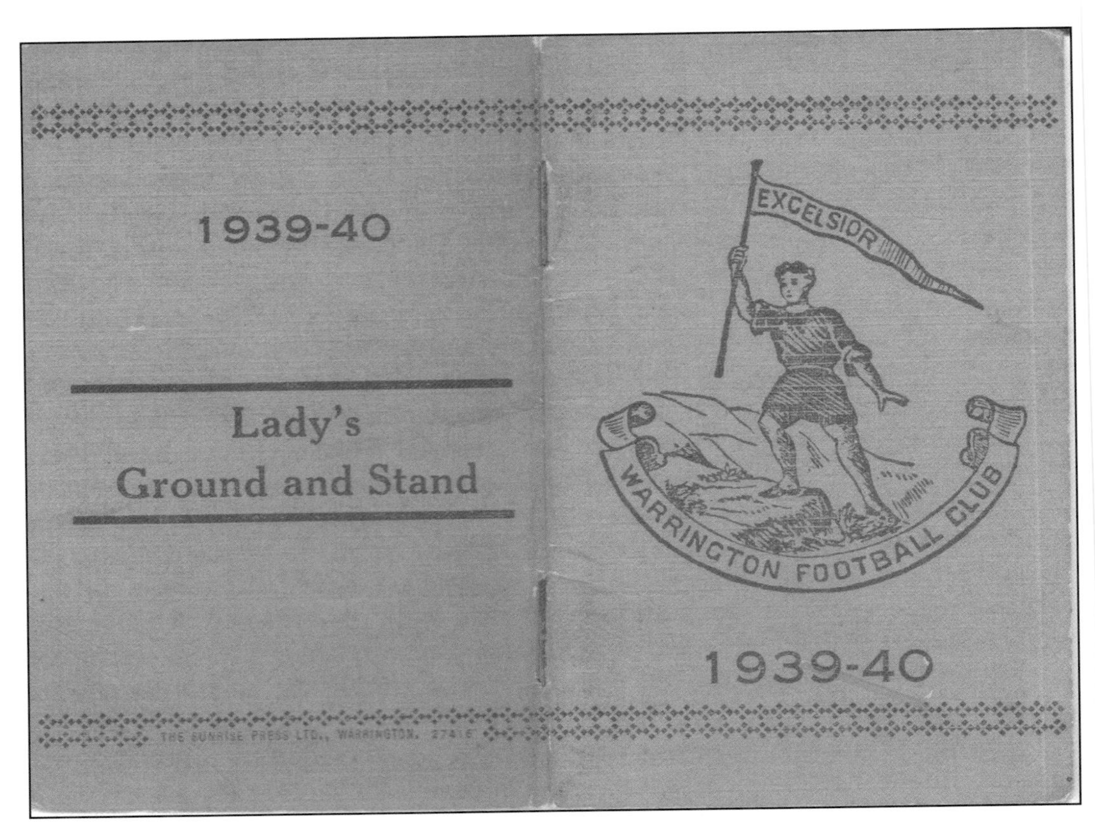

A lady's ground and stand season ticket for the 1939-40 season, complete with Excelsior badge.

Left: Warrington stand-off Mel de Lloyd was suspended indefinitely after punching the referee while playing for Keighley in January 1942. Right: Albert Johnson made his debut in January 1939 after playing some trial games under the pseudonym Pilkington.

Warrington Football Club

The Government has made a request that as many Football Clubs as possible should "carry on" for the entertainment of the Troops and the Public, so the Committee of the Warrington Football Club have given long and earnest consideration to the position. We have now decided that we will make an effort to provide Football this season, and we ask our members and the sporting public to do all they can to make the season a successful one.

In order to reduce the Bank Overdraft and to ensure funds for starting the season properly, we have decided to issue Season Tickets, AVAILABLE TO EVERYBODY, at the following prices :— **MEN, 10/-; LADIES, 7/6; BOYS, 5/-,**

These tickets include admission to the Grandstand, and will be available for all League Matches, but not for Cup Ties.

We must, however, point out that the number of our players is very limited, and will be still further depleted as other players are called up for the Services, and there is, therefore, a **possibility** that we shall not be able to carry the game on right through the season, and Purchasers of Season Tickets must understand that they take the risk of this occurring.

At the same time, we appeal to all friends of sport in this district to assist the Club by taking out Tickets and persuading friends to do likewise, or to encourage them to attend the Matches as much as possible.

The Season Tickets will be on sale at the Football Field on Match Days, and can also be obtained at any time at :—

R. APPLETON, Newsagent, RYLANDS STREET.
THE SPORTS CENTRE, SANKEY STREET.
THE ORFORD HOTEL, GORSEY LANE.
THE BLACKBURN ARMS, MARKET PLACE.
THE WHITE HART HOTEL, SANKEY STREET.
WARRINGTON TYRE HOUSE, SANKEY STREET.
or From any Member of the Committee.

TEAM SHEETS

Official Team Sheets will be issued whenever possible and sent through the post as follows :—

One Copy, 3/-; Two Copies, 3/6; Three Copies, 4/-; and can be obtained on application to R. F. ANDERTON, White Hart Hotel.

PLAYERS

The Committee invite any Rugby players who would like to play for our Club to communicate with our Team Manager, Mr. C. BROCKBANK, 6, Algernon Street, Stockton Heath, Warrington.

The Government urged clubs to carry on playing to provide entertainment for the troops and the public.

Force. The last match at Wilderspool before the ground was requisitioned was on 28 December 1940 when Warrington beat Oldham 19-2.

After that, the club was effectively mothballed and any Warrington players who wanted to continue playing had to guest for other clubs. The pay was not great – it was set at 10/0d – but there were other benefits. Hooker Dave Cotton, for example, once received a parcel of fresh fish as a win bonus and, at a time of food rationing, that would have been most welcome. Billy Belshaw and Ossie Peake turned out for Huddersfield for most of the 1941-42 season and Peake finished the campaign with 26 tries.

Stand-off Mel de Lloyd guested for Keighley in the 1941-42 season, but soon found himself immersed in controversy. On 3 January, during a match against Hull, the Welshman was sent off for disputing a decision with the referee and then hit the unfortunate official. De Lloyd was suspended sine die (indefinitely), although the ban was lifted 10 months later.

Frank Gregory, Warrington's former England second-row forward, enjoyed more success with Leeds and was a member of the team which won the Challenge Cup in 1942 by beating Halifax 15-10 in the Final at Odsal. Gregory, like Tommy Blinkhorn before him, became a professional wrestler when his rugby league-playing days were over. He was still competing at Warrington Baths on Monday 20 October 1958, in a bout which was promoted in the usual enthusiastic manner: "Francis St Clair Gregory (Redruth). The ex-Warrington and Wigan prop-forward, eight times Cornish champion; one of the roughest mat men in the game" was pitted against "Massambula (West Africa). The only wrestling witch doctor – don't miss this unique grappler whose novel style has made him the ace wrestler of the year."

The match-up was described in advance as a "sensational heavyweight clash of the giants" but did not quite live up to its billing. The *Warrington Guardian* reported: "The crowd were disappointed at the display of Gregory. The bout ended with referee Stan Rylance disqualifying the Cornishman in the fifth round for persistent fouling."

Warrington, however, were facing financial problems. With no gate money coming in, few bills could be paid and so a meeting was held at the British Legion Cub in June 1942. Members decided to turn the club into a limited liability company with share capital of £10,000 – Warrington Football Club Ltd was born. A number of shares were held back for members who were in the forces, but nearly £3,000 was raised to help the club over its difficulties.

Also in 1942, Warrington director Bob Anderton was elected chairman of the Rugby League Council – a post he held for three years. There was some opposition from Huddersfield, who felt that only competing clubs should have members on the game's emergency committee. Their opposition melted away, however, when it was argued that it was difficult enough to find able administrators without introducing such restrictions.

2ND NEW ZEALAND EXPEDITIONARY FORCE

ONWARD

10649 Lieutenant Rex Keith King

It was with the greatest pleasure that I read in Army Orders that you had been awarded the Military Cross for gallant and distinguished service in the field, and I wish to send you my personal congratulations.

In the field,

January 15th 1942

B. Freyberg

Major-General,
Commanding New Zealand Division
2nd N.Z.E.F.

NZ

ONWARD

New Zealander Rex King was awarded the Military Cross.

More common sense was shown when the Rugby Football Union briefly put their hatred of rugby league on hold for the greater good and allowed two rugby league versus rugby union games - under union rules - to be staged, to raise money for wartime charities. Bill Chapman, the Warrington loose-forward, played in both.

The first, between the Northern Command League XV and the Northern Command Union XV, was held at Headingley on Saturday 23 January 1943. The league team won 18-11 in front of 8,000 spectators. How Private Chapman must have enjoyed that.

The experiment was repeated at Odsal on 24 April the following year by which time Chapman was a sergeant. Again the league men won, 15-10. This was to be the last cross-code skirmish for 52 years, until Wigan and Bath played each other at Maine Road and Twickenham in 1996.

Prop-forward Jack 'Cod' Miller had appeared in three losing Challenge Cup Final teams for Warrington – in 1928, 1933 and 1936 – but in 1945, while guesting for Huddersfield, he finally got his hands on a winner's medal.

Jack Arkwright (first right), Dave Cotton (standing fourth left) and Billy Belshaw (kneeling centre) all won Lancashire county caps during the 1938-39 season. All three players returned to Wilderspool after the war.

Huddersfield, with Miller in the pack and Ossie Peake on the wing, won both legs of the final against Bradford Northern, 7-4 at home and 6-5 away.

Inevitably, of course, the war also brought the worst of news. Flying officer Frank Cueto, the Warrington scrum-half, was killed in action in February 1944 when his RAF fighter plane went down over the English Channel. He was just 27. Cueto had made 79 appearances from 1936 to 1940, scoring 10 tries, and was a member of the 1937 Lancashire Cup-winning side. He had already represented his native Cumberland and had been tipped as a future Great Britain scrum-half. He had so much to live for.

For Warrington, the period after the war did – eventually – produce glory, with both the Championship and the Challenge Cup finally arriving at Wilderspool. The club also participated in one of the game's most famous matches, the 1954 Challenge Cup Final replay at Odsal. The patience of players and fans in the 1920s and 1930s was finally rewarded.

Appendix: Statistics and records

Leading try scorers

1914-15: Jim Tranter (11)
1915-16: Did not play
1916-17: Jim Baker (9)
1917-18: Sam Lloyd (12)
1918-19: Jim Tranter (9)
1919-20: Jim Tranter (7)
1920-21: Arthur Skelhorn (10)
1921-22: Jim Tranter (15)
1922-23: Dickie Blackburn & Jim Tranter (12)
1923-24: Dickie Blackburn & Jim Tranter (16)
1924-25: Dickie Blackburn (15)
1925-26: Billy Roberts (21)
1926-27: Tommy Flynn (22)
1927-28: Billy Rhodes (22)
1928-29: Billy Dingsdale (28) to equal club record set by Jack Fish in 1909-10
1929-30: Billy Dingsdale (25)
1930-31: Tommy Thompson (28) to equal above club record
1931-32: Bill Shankland (23)
1932-33: Steve Ray (33) new club record
1933-34: Tommy Thompson & Jack Garrett (15)
1934-35: Jack Garrett (20)
1935-36: Ben Hawker (15)
1936-37: Griff Jenkins (16)
1937-38: Dave Brown (20)
1938-39: Izzy Davies (34) new club record
1939-40: Eli Dixon (13)
1940-41: Billy Belshaw, Eli Dixon & Ossie Peake (11)

Leading goalkickers (including drop-goals)

1914-15: Ben Jolley (20)
1915-16: Did not play
1916-17: Ben Jolley (24)
1917-18: Sam Lloyd (12)
1918-19: William Potter (14)
1919-20: Ben Jolley (23)
1920-21: Arthur Fowles (34)
1921-22: Ben Jolley (53) new club record
1922-23: Tom Mannion (18)
1923-24: Ben Jolley (25)
1924-25: Ben Jolley (44)
1925-26: Ben Jolley (54) new club record
1926-27: Ned Catterall (27)
1927-28: Billy Rhodes (32)
1928-29: Billy Rhodes (40)
1929-30: Billy Holding (84) new club record
1930-31: Billy Holding (101) new club record
1931-32: Billy Holding (92)
1932-33: Billy Holding (125) new club record
1933-34: Billy Holding (116)
1934-35: Billy Holding (73)
1935-36: Billy Holding (67)
1936-37: Billy Holding (70)
1937-38: Billy Holding (60)
1938-39: Billy Belshaw (47)
1939-40: Billy Belshaw (52)
1940-41: Billy Belshaw (27)

Leading point scorers

1914-15: Ernie Brookes (56)
1915-16: Did not play
1916-17: Ben Jolley (60)
1917-18: Sam Lloyd (60)
1918-19: William Potter (37)
1919-20: Ben Jolley (49)
1920-21: Arthur Fowles (68)
1921-22: Ben Jolley (106)
1922-23: Tom Mannion (39)
1923-24: Ned Catterall & Ben Jolley (50)
1924-25: Ned Catterall (107)
1925-26: Ben Jolley (108)
1926-27: Tommy Flynn (98)
1927-28: Billy Rhodes (130)
1928-29: Tommy Blinkhorn (114)
1929-30: Billy Holding (168) new club record
1930-31: Billy Holding (205) new club record
1931-32: Billy Holding (184)
1932-33: Billy Holding (256) new club record
1933-34: Billy Holding (238)
1934-35: Billy Holding (146)
1935-36: Billy Holding (137)
1936-37: Billy Holding (140)
1937-38: Dave Brown (132)
1938-39: Dave Brown (144)
1939-40: Billy Belshaw (122)
1940-41: Billy Belshaw (87)

Ever-present in a season

1916-17: Jim Tranter (30 apps)
1925-26: Freddie Ryder (42)
1926-27: Alf Peacock (41)
1928-29: Tommy Flynn & Les Perkins (44)
1929-30: Tommy Blinkhorn (44)
1934-35: Rex King (43)
1936-37: Dave Cotton (44)
1937-38: Dave Brown (42)
1940-41: Dave Cotton & Les Jones (16)

Hat-trick of tries on debut

Bill Stockley versus Bradford Northern at Wilderspool on 4 October 1924
Izzy Davies versus Leigh at Leigh on 17 March 1937

Five tries in a match

Steve Ray versus Wigan Highfield at Wilderspool on 4 March 1933
Izzy Davies versus Leigh at Wilderspool on 17 April 1939

Six tries in a match

Tommy Thompson v Bradford Northern at Wilderspool on 6 April 1933

Testimonials

1919-20: Arthur Naylor & Ernie Jordan
1921-22: Jim Daintith & George Thomas' widow
1924-25: Arthur Skelhorn & Jim Tranter
1925-26: Ben Jolley & Jim Fearnley
1927-28: Tom & Billy Cunliffe
1929-30: Alf Peacock
1932-33: Frank Mason & Frank Williams
1937-38: Jack Miller & Sam Hardman
1938-39: Billy Holding

Record transfer fees paid

£100 to Hull KR for Jack Prescott in August 1919.
£300 to Oldham for Jerry Donovan in November 1923.
£400 to St Helens for Tommy Flynn in December 1925.
£650 to Broughton Rangers for Dai Davies in November 1927.
£700 to St Helens for Jack Arkwright in September 1934.
£1,450 to Liverpool Stanley for Billy Belshaw in October 1937.

Representative honours

Great Britain tourists

1920: Billy Cunliffe & Arthur Skelhorn
1924: Billy Cunliffe
1932: Billy Dingsdale
1936: Jack Arkwright & Jack Miller

Great Britain

Jack Arkwright (6) 1936 to 1937
Billy Belshaw (2) 1937
Nat Bentham (2) 1929
Tommy Blinkhorn (1) 1929
Billy Cunliffe (11) 1920 to 1926
Billy Dingsdale (3) 1929 to 1933
Jack Miller (6) 1933 to 1936
Arthur Skelhorn (7) 1920 to 1921

England

Jack Arkwright (4) 1936 to 1938
Billy Belshaw (8) 1938 to 1945
Nat Bentham (2) 1930
Tommy Blinkhorn (1) 1929
Billy Cunliffe (10) 1921 to 1926
Billy Dingsdale (7) 1928 to 1933
Frank Gregory (1) 1939
Billy Kirk (1) 1930
Jack Miller (4) 1928 to 1936
Alf Peacock (1) 1925
Ossie Peake (3) 1939 to 1941
Arthur Skelhorn (3) 1921-23
Tommy Thompson (1) 1933
Jim Tranter (2) 1922-23
Frank Williams (1) 1930

Wales

Bill Chapman (2) 1943 to 1944
Dai Davies (4) 1928 to 1935
Ponty Davies (1) 1928
Mel de Lloyd (1) 1945
Arthur Evans (1) 1933
Tommy Flynn (1) 1930
Jesse Meredith (1) 1930
Steve Ray (1) 1932

Other Nationalities
Dai Davies (1) 1930
Jesse Meredith (1) 1930
Bill Shankland (1) 1933

Lancashire
Jack Arkwright (8) 1935 to 1938
Billy Belshaw (6) 1938 to 1946
Nat Bentham (4) 1930
Dave Cotton (1) 1938
Billy Cunliffe (19) 1918 to 1927
Billy Dingsdale (14) 1928 to 1933
Sam Hardman (1) 1932
Ben Jolley (4) 1913 to 1920
Bill Jones (2) 1932
Billy Kirk (2) 1930
Jack Miller (3) 1933 to 1936
Alf Peacock (1) 1925
Ossie Peake (2) 1938
Arthur Skelhorn (6) 1919 to 1922
Bob Smith (2) 1933
Jim Tranter (8) 1919 to 1925
Frank Williams (1) 1927

Cumberland
Bob Beattie (2) 1930 to 1931
Frank Cueto (3) 1937 to 1938
Billy Holding (14) 1929 to 1938

Glamorgan & Monmouthshire
Dai Davies (5) 1929 to 1931
Ponty Davies (1) 1927
Tommy Flynn (4) 1927 to 1931
Jesse Meredith (3) 1929 to 1930
Les Perkins (1) 1930
Billy Rhodes (1) 1927

Monmouthshire
Tommy Flynn (1) 1927
Billy Rhodes (1) 1927

Yorkshire
Jim Marsden (1) 1931

Player records

Name	Debut	Last Game	App	T	G	DG	Pts	Pen Picture
Abbott, Norman	25/04/25		1	0	0	0	0	Centre signed from Wigan Old Boys (OB) RUFC.
Anderson, Tommy	19/2/21	18/4/22	39	2	0	0	6	Scrum-half. 1921 Lancashire Cup winner.
Arkwright snr, Jack	29/9/34	8/9/45	164	30	3	1	98	Second-row. 6GB caps. Hall of Fame. Oldest player aged 42.
Armstrong, A.	20/3/28	24/3/28	2	0	0	0	0	Winger. One game on each wing.
Arnold, James	27/8/27	12/11/27	10	0	0	0	0	Scrum-half. Signed from Swinton.
Arrowsmith, Charlie	14/3/25	26/11/27	8	1	0	0	3	Loose-forward from Wigan OB RUFC. Only try versus Salford.
Ashton, Ernie	11/12/26	10/4/28	2	0	0	0	0	Winger. Played in record 68-14 defeat at Hunslet in April 1928.
Ashton, Harry	25/3/22	10/11/23	39	2	0	1	8	Stand-off. Signed from Crosfields. 27 apps in 1922-23 season.
Aspey, G.	31/8/35	7/9/35	3	0	0	0	0	Prop-forward.
Bailey,	26/12/24		1	0	0	0	0	Second-row forward. Only appearance at Rochdale.
Baker, John	26/11/27	28/1/28	3	0	0	0	0	Winger signed after scoring four tries in 'A' team.
Banner, John Edward	31/1/20	6/3/20	5	0	0	0	0	Left winger. Played five games in a row.
Baron,	1/2/19		1	0	0	0	0	Scrum-half. Only match an 8-3 defeat at St Helens.
Barton, Joseph	23/10/20	25/3/21	10	0	0	0	0	Prop or second-row-forward.
Baxter, Bill	16/9/33	7/5/36	19	0	5	0	10	Full-back from Leigh. Reserve for 1936 Challenge Cup Final.
Beattie, Bob	4/9/30	5/12/31	20	3	0	0	9	Cumbrian half-back from Wigan OB RUFC.

Belshaw, Billy	30/10/37	9/3/46	132	29	167	5	431	Full-back / centre / stand-off. Record signing, £1,450
Bennett, Fred	1/3/30		1	0	0	0	0	Half-back.
Bennett, Ivor	28/8/37	9/11/46	73	13	0	0	39	Welsh second row from Aberavon. 1937 Lancashire Cup winner.
Bentham, Nat	11/1/30	11/5/35	202	2	0	0	6	Hooker signed from Halifax.
Bevan, Dai	28/9/12	25/9/20	16	0	0	0	0	Second-row forward.
Blackburn, Dickie	27/8/21	18/4/27	169	65	0	0	195	Right winger in 1926 Championship Final vs Wigan.
Blinkhorn, Tommy	1/12/28	6/5/33	126	52	36	0	228	Winger. Played in 1933 Cup Final.
Booth, James	10/1/20		1	0	0	0	0	Hooker. Only match 18-0 defeat at Rochdale.
Bradbury, Bob	27/11/20	7/10/22	57	19	0	0	57	Winger. Scored only try in 1921 Lancashire Cup win
Brennan, William	16/10/20	27/8/21	28	0	0	0	0	Hooker signed from St Helens Recs. Later joined Batley.
Brindle, Walter	6/3/26	24/3/28	4	0	0	0	0	Centre / winger. Made debut at Swinton.
Brockbank, William	24/4/20	18/9/20	5	0	0	0	0	Left centre. Debut against Wigan at home
Brookes, Ernie	22/11/02	20/3/20	297	81	25	0	293	Stand-off. Called "The Terrier" for his strength.
Brown, Dave	23/1/37	29/4/39	93	48	91	0	326	Prolific Australian centre. Two tries in 1937 Lancashire Cup win.
Brown, K.	19/10/35	26/10/35	2	0	0	0	0	Prop-forward. Made debut at Liverpool Stanley.
Butler, Lol	26/2/31	1/1/34	2	0	0	0	0	Scrum-half.
Butler, T.	8/2/19	3/5/19	4	1	0	0	3	Half-back. Try-scoring debut versus St Helens at home.
Callan, Stan	5/9/21	2/1/22	13	1	0	0	3	Stand-off. Scored only try versus Wakefield at home.
Carey, James	25/1/19	1/2/19	2	0	0	0	0	Centre / stand-off from the Wigan district.
Cartwright, Bert	28/8/20	7/4/23	84	18	0	0	54	Winger from Wigan Highfield. Played in 1921 Lancashire Cup win.
Catterall, Ned	9/2/24	4/12/26	101	15	134	0	313	Centre signed from Wakefield. Sold to Bradford Northern.
Chadwick, Jack	17/11/34	16/11/40	82	8	0	0	24	Loose-forward at Wembley in 1936. Sold to Halifax.
Chamberlain, W.	15/2/19	12/4/19	6	1	0	0	3	Forward from Wigan district. Try-scoring debut versus Oldham.
Chapman, Bill	31/8/35	4/1/47	179	27	0	0	81	Welsh loose-forward from Bridgend. 1937 Lancashire Cup winner.
Child, Arthur	19/11/23	13/2/26	74	18	0	0	54	Welsh centre. Career ended by a broken thigh.
Clarke, Thomas	25/1/19	5/3/21	77	1	0	0	3	Forward. Only try versus Broughton Rangers at home.
Clegg, John	15/2/19		1	0	0	0	0	Forward. Only match versus Oldham at home.
Close, Jack	13/11/26	10/4/28	13	0	5	0	10	Full-back signed from Wigan Highfield.
Collins, Charlie	15/1/21	9/12/22	18	0	0	0	0	Centre. Dislocated shoulder in 1921 Lancashire Cup Final win.
Connolly, Len	10/4/28	12/9/31	4	1	0	0	3	Forward signed from local ARL. Made debut in record defeat.
Connor, W.	12/12/25		1	0	0	0	0	Prop. Only game 7-7 draw versus Oldham.

Cotton, Dave	2/11/35	13/11/48	326	9	0	0	27	Veteran hooker in the 1947-48 Championship-winning side.
Cox, George	22/11/22	14/4/23	24	0	0	0	0	Second row signed from Ebbw Vale.
Cueto, Frank	31/10/36	7/9/40	79	10	0	0	30	Scrum-half from Stockton Heath. Killed in action in February 1944.
Cunliffe, Billy	17/10/14	6/9/30	438	38	6	0	126	Prop. GB tourist in 1920 & 1924.
Cunliffe, Tom	19/12/14	24/11/28	324	48	0	0	144	Forward. Billy's younger brother. Joint testimonial in 1927-28.
Daintith, Jim 'Shint'	8/2/08	16/3/21	155	12	7	2	54	Warrington-born scrum-half in 1913 Challenge Cup Final team.
Daniel, S H	28/8/20		1	0	0	0	0	Left winger on opening day of the 1920-21 season.
Davies, D.	18/9/20		1	0	0	0	0	Stand-off. Only match in 26-6 defeat at St Helens.
Davies, Dai Morgan	26/11/27	3/11/34	196	34	0	0	102	Cocky Welsh scrum-half. Four-time Challenge Cup Final loser.
Davies, Fred	10/1/20	3/4/20	4	0	0	0	0	Stand-off / loose-forward.
Davies, Harold	10/1/20	5/4/20	6	1	0	0	3	Half-back. Served in South Lancs regiment in World War 1.
Davies, Izzy	17/3/37	26/12/39	69	57	0	0	171	Winger. Leading try scorer in 1938-39 with 34 in 35 matches.
Davies, 'Ponty'	10/9/27	17/11/28	39	0	0	0	0	Second-row signed from Pontypridd RLFC.
Dawson, J.	19/12/31	5/3/32	13	3	0	0	9	Second-row signed from Balmoral RUFC (Ormskirk).
de Lloyd, Mel	26/9/36	4/10/47	176	24	27	7	140	Welsh stand-off. Lancashire Cup winner in 1937.
Dennett, Harry	13/3/29	22/11/30	6	0	0	0	0	Winger / centre.
Dickenson, Jim	3/9/23	16/4/28	19	1	0	0	3	Half-back from local ARL. Only try in record defeat at Hunslet.
Dilorenzo, Vin	19/3/32	16/3/40	18	0	0	0	0	Warrington-born hooker. Also played for Bradford and St Helens.
Dingsdale, Ben	3/3/28	24/11/28	9	0	0	0	0	Winger / centre. Billy's brother.
Dingsdale, Billy	15/9/28	18/5/40	373	154	4	0	470	Clever centre. 1932 tour. Hall of Fame.
Dixon, Eli	26/8/39	21/9/46	41	25	11	1	99	Stand-off / centre. Signed from St Helens Recs.
Donovan, Jerry	1/12/23	8/9/24	30	5	0	2	19	Scrum-half signed from Oldham for £300. Sold to Keighley.
Dover, Tommy	24/11/28	12/12/31	12	0	0	0	0	Forward.
Downes, Harry	27/8/32	3/9/32	2	0	0	0	0	Centre signed from Leigh (20 appearances from 1930-32).
Dumbell, Jack	18/1/19		1	0	0	0	0	Forward signed from Rylands.
Edge, Alf	30/3/37	23/3/40	46	1	0	0	3	Prop-forward. Only try versus Broughton. At Leigh 1948-49.
Edlestone, Will	22/2/19		1	0	0	0	0	Right centre. Only game at St Helens Recs.
Edwards	16/12/22		1	0	0	0	0	Pseudonym for a Welsh trialist centre versus Leeds
Edwards, J.	24/12/38	4/11/39	6	0	0	0	0	Forward.
Evans, Arthur 'Candy'	26/9/31	10/11/34	109	21	0	0	63	Giant Welsh second row in 1933 Challenge Cup Final.
Evans, Stanley	20/10/28	25/10/28	2	0	0	0	0	Winger. Signed from the Rastrick ARLFC in Halifax League.
Fearnley, Jim 'Scuddy'	2/12/11	1/11/24	204	39	0	1	119	Forward in 1913 Challenge Cup Final. Testimonial 1925-26.
Fearnley, William	1/2/19		1	0	0	0	0	Winger. Only game 8-3 defeat at St Helens.

Fisher, John	7/12/29	25/12/29	5	0	0	0	0	Hooker in 1929 victory over Australia. Moved to Swinton.
Flannery, Mick	2/11/35	19/9/36	31	0	8	0	16	Signed from Leigh. Second row in 1936 Challenge Cup Final.
Floyd, Gwynne	21/1/39	22/4/39	11	5	0	0	15	Centre signed from Maesteg RU.
Flynn, Tommy	12/12/25	20/4/32	224	73	42	7	317	Welsh stand-off signed from St Helens. Became groundsman.
Forrest, Bill	31/8/1935	26/10/35	4	0	0	0	0	Hooker. Lost his place in the team to Dave Cotton.
Forsyth, W.	29/4/39		1	0	0	0	0	Hooker. Played versus Oldham on last day of 1938-39 season.
Foster,	18/1/19	25/1/19	2	0	0	0	0	Winger in games at Widnes and Wigan. Played two, lost two.
Fowles, Arthur	13/3/20	30/9/22	35	0	51	0	102	Full-back. Could kick ball huge distances. Nicknamed Farmer.
French, Freddie	30/11/35		1	0	0	0	0	Kiwi full-back who later enjoyed success at Barrow.
Friend, B.	28/12/35	13/4/36	2	0	0	0	0	Hooker.
Frowen, Arthur	6/9/24	1/10/32	183	12	8	3	58	Full-back. Ferocious tackler. Played in 1928 Challenge Cup Final.
Gabriel, Tom	29/11/24	31/1/25	3	0	0	0	0	Centre / full-back.
Gallop, J.U.	18/1/19	3/5/19	4	1	0	0	3	Scrum-half. Only try against Oldham at home
Garrett, Harry	16/9/36	19/9/36	2	0	0	0	0	Stand-off. Jack's brother.
Garrett, Jack	28/11/31	5/10/40	193	77	0	0	231	Warrington-born winger in 1936 Challenge Cup Final.
Gautrey, Reg	16/1/26	11/9/26	11	2	0	0	6	Centre signed from Rugby RUFC.
Gibson, David	20/3/20		1	0	0	0	0	Centre. Only match a 14-12 defeat at Salford.
Gifford, Reg	1/2/19	11/9/20	12	2	0	0	6	Left centre.
Goodall, Jack	10/11/34	28/12/40	146	22	0	2	70	Scrum-half in 3 major finals (1935, 36 & 37). All were lost.
Gormley, Thomas	18/1/19	5/4/19	12	1	0	0	3	Winger. Made a try-scoring debut at Widnes.
Goulden, J.	23/4/38	19/11/38	3	0	0	0	0	Hooker.
Green, Jack	30/8/26	14/1/28	41	7	0	0	21	Centre sold to Broughton Rangers.
Green, Mark	6/9/13	13/9/19	53	2	0	0	6	Forward. Capped for Lancashire.
Gregory, Francis	5/2/38	2/3/46	79	6	0	0	18	Cornish forward. Became professional wrestler.
Griffin, Tom	3/3/34	10/11/34	15	2	0	0	6	Loose-forward.
Griffith, H.	5/3/21		1	0	0	0	0	Stand-off in 15-0 defeat vs Halifax at Wilderspool.
Griffith, J.	25/12/31	16/12/33	18	1	0	0	3	Prop-forward signed from Pleasley Cross ARLFC.
Griffiths, J.B.	21/12/29	14/4/30	10	1	0	0	3	Cardiff RU stand-off. Debut in famous victory over Australia.
Grounds, Syd	8/2/19		1	1	0	0	3	Winger. Discovered playing for Warrington Butchers in 1913.
Halfpenny, Ben	26/1/35	16/2/35	5	1	0	0	3	Prop / second row. Scored try in 18-5 win at Leigh.
Halsall, J.	23/11/35	14/3/36	3	0	0	0	0	Centre. Played three, lost three.
Hanley, M.	7/10/22	21/10/22	3	0	0	0	0	Stand-off. Features in Pinnace cigarette card collection.
Hardman, Sammy	10/4/28	29/1/38	200	7	0	0	21	Prop in 1933 and 1936 Challenge Cup Finals. Testimonial 1937-38.
Hardy, Bill 'Nelson'	29/8/31	26/12/33	38	5	0	0	15	Australian test centre signed from Eastern Suburbs.
Harrop, Bill	26/1/25	30/4/27	80	2	0	0	6	Prop signed from Devonport Services RUFC.

Hassall, Arthur	03/9/21	7/1/22	4	0	0	0	0	Winger. Product of Warrington's 'A' team.
Hawker, Ben	30/12/33	17/12/38	88	30	0	0	90	Welsh centre in 1936 Cup Final. Later murdered his wife.
Haywood, Joe	6/9/19	24/4/20	22	3	0	0	9	Winger signed from Manchester United FC. Sold to Widnes.
Hazelhurst, Roy	23/11/35	22/4/36	10	0	0	0	0	Stand-off / full-back from Canterbury RU, New Zealand.
Heesom, Syd	16/9/33	13/4/36	37	3	0	0	9	Stand-off from Warrington RU. Reserve for 1936 Challenge Cup Final.
Hewitt, A.E.	1/1/36	6/2/37	9	2	0	0	6	Winger sold to Leigh where he played 30 games in 1938-39.
Higginbottom, Fred	26/8/39	23/8/47	90	19	53	0	163	Centre signed from Rylands. Played in Bevan's first game.
Hodgetts, Don	13/9/30	13/4/31	13	0	0	0	0	Right wing / centre signed from Old Widnesians RUFC
Holding, Billy	21/1/28	9/11/40	328	6	830	4	1,686	Cumbrian full-back. First Wire to kick 100 goals in a season.
Holland, Charles	19/9/25	17/10/25	5	1	0	0	3	Stand-off. Only try in 5-0 win at Oldham.
Hollins, J.	29/9/34	13/4/36	3	0	0	0	0	Half-back.
Hollinsworth, G.	27/8/32	23/3/40	34	3	0	0	9	Second-row forward. Signed from Scholes, Wigan junior team.
Hopkins, W.	21/4/28	20/4/29	6	1	0	0	3	Left wing / second row. Scored only try at Dewsbury.
Jones, Ron	30/8/26	24/12/27	31	9	18	0	63	Centre signed from Forest of Dean RUFC.
King, Rex	25/8/34	13/2/37	76	29	0	0	87	New Zealand loose-forward. Won Military Cross for bravery.
Kirk, Billy	19/11/27	30/3/34	102	16	0	0	48	Scrum-half. Carried off injured in 1928 Challenge Cup Final.
Lavin, Bill	25/9/20	21/1/22	34	3	0	0	9	Centre signed from St Helens. 30 games in 1920-21.
Laws, Tommy	5/9/14	6/3/20	42	4	0	0	12	Half-back / centre. Played friendlies in 1917-18.
Lees, Harry	2/4/26		1	0	0	0	0	Full-back signed from Oldham RUFC.
Leyland, W.H.	4/10/24	25/9/26	39	2	0	0	6	Second-row signed from Wigan OB RUFC.
Lloyd, Samual	12/4/19	24/1/20	20	1	0	0	3	Winger. Scored only try in 13-12 win at Oldham in May 1919.
Loughlin, P.	16/10/37		1	0	0	0	0	Hooker against Leeds in one of Dave Cotton's rare absences.
Makin, Eddie	25/12/22	3/10/25	22	8	0	0	24	Winger. Product of Warrington's 'A' team.
Mannion, Tom	23/9/22	7/4/23	20	1	18	0	39	Centre from Barrow. Featured in Pinnace cigarette cards.
Marsden, Jim	29/11/30	18/4/33	63	10	0	1	32	Yorkshire county second-row signed from Dewsbury.
Mason,	14/1/39	8/9/45	3	0	0	0	0	Back-row forward.
Mason, Frank	27/12/21	11/4/31	105	7	0	0	21	Centre turned second row-forward. Testimonial in 1932-33.
Mather, Robert	3/10/14	16/9/22	71	1	0	0	3	Prop in 1921 Lancashire Cup win. Only try at Runcorn.
Matthews, Will	16/4/21		1	0	0	0	0	Right centre at Swinton on the last day of 1920-21 season.
Maxfield, (trialist)	19/4/27		1	0	0	0	0	Pseudonym used by a Welsh centre.

McNulty, Frank	28/8/20	24/11/23	65	10	3	0	36	Scrum-half signed from Wigan Highfield.
Meredith, Jesse	17/10/27	25/4/31	113	9	1	1	31	Welsh centre / second row. Played in 1928 Challenge Cup Final.
Miller, Jack 'Cod'	11/12/26	9/2/46	526	31	0	0	93	Prop. 1936 tour. Hall of Fame.
Mitchell, Harry	1/1/34		1	0	0	0	0	Winger signed from New Springs ARLFC.
Moon, Bill	27/12/27		1	0	0	0	0	Prop-forward. Only game against Wigan Highfield.
Morley, Ellis	21/1/22	4/12/26	6	0	0	0	0	Forward.
Morris, J.	4/9/26	9/9/26	2	1	0	0	3	Pseudonym given to a trialist winger from Midlands RU club
Mulhall, Alec	4/11/39	31/1/48	20	1	0	0	3	Forward. Transferred to Keighley.
Newcomb, Jimmy	12/12/31	18/2/39	135	20	2	4	72	Stand-off in 1936 Challenge Cup Final at Wembley.
Nicholas, Syd	19/10/12	18/10/19	71	6	21	0	60	Stand-off in 1913 Challenge Cup Final team.
Nicholls, Tom	28/3/14	28/1/22	18	5	2	0	19	Winger. Five tries in 14 appearances in 1920-21.
Norris, Walter	11/2/39	14/9/46	26	1	0	0	3	Forward signed from Rylands. Moved to St Helens in 1947.
Ogden, George	10/9/21	11/11/22	47	0	0	0	0	Second rower in the 1921 Lancashire Cup win. Transferred to Leigh.
O'Rourke, J.	25/12/30	3/9/32	4	1	0	0	3	Winger signed from Orford Tannery. Only try versus Broughton.
Oster, Jackie	27/8/32	9/9/33	40	4	0	2	16	Signed from Oldham. Stand-off in 1933 Challenge Cup Final.
Owen, E.	1/11/23	17/11/23	5	0	0	0	0	Half-back.
Palin, Harold 'Moggy'	22/2/36	23/4/51	150	32	436	3	974	Loose-forward. Captain of 47-48 championship-winning side.
Parker, Dai	2/10/37	4/3/39	16	0	0	1	2	Scrum-half signed from Neath RUFC.
Parry, Jack	2/10/26	7/4/28	36	7	0	0	21	Winger.
Peacock, Alf	23/8/19	23/11/29	367	10	0	0	30	Club's first specialist hooker. Wore skull cap.
Peake, Ossie	2/4/38	13/11/48	118	48	0	0	144	Centre from Newton Grammar School.
Percival, Frank	31/12/21	7/4/23	2	0	1	0	2	Full-back signed from Crosfields.
Perkins, Les	8/10/27	19/3/34	176	48	2	3	154	Welsh centre. Captain of the 1929 Lancashire Cup winners.
Phibbs, James	27/8/21		1	0	0	0	0	Hooker against Broughton on opening day of 1921-22 season.
Pierce, W.	17/11/23	21/11/25	5	2	0	0	6	Stand-off.
Potter, Fred	18/1/19	5/4/20	19	4	0	0	12	Centre/forward. Played in first game after the First World War.
Potter, William	18/1/19	6/9/20	31	5	28	0	71	Stand-off / centre. Played in first game after First World War.
Prescott, Jack	28/8/20	27/12/21	50	7	0	0	21	Stand-off. Captain of club's first Lancashire Cup winners in 1921.
Rankin, Bill	18/4/30	28/8/37	75	1	6	0	15	Prop in 1937 Championship Final defeat. Sold to Rochdale.
Ray, Steve	30/1/32	30/12/33	64	45	0	0	135	Winger. Leading try-scorer in 1932-33 with 33 in 44 matches.
Redmond, Chris	3/2/23	15/3/24	35	3	10	0	29	Former Widnes centre featured in Pinnace cigarette cards.
Rees, Rhys	2/2/24	24/1/25	30	5	0	0	15	Centre signed from Hull KR.
Rhodes, Billy	18/12/26	30/3/29	80	31	73	0	239	Centre / winger signed from Pontypridd.

Roberts, B.	27/8/21	5/9/21	3	0	0	0	0	Winger in three defeats at start of 1921-22 season.
Roberts, T.W. 'Fanny'	6/12/24	18/1/30	117	54	0	0	162	Winger in 1926 Championship Final defeat. 21 tries that season.
Robinson, A.T.	24/9/21	27/3/26	70	6	0	0	18	Back-row forward. Product of Warrington's 'A' team.
Robinson, Harry	21/2/20	9/10/20	16	2	0	0	6	Loose-forward.
Robinson, J.	25/3/32	15/10/32	11	1	0	0	3	Centre. Only try in 30-15 win versus Wigan at home
Robinson, W.	3/10/25	23/1/26	2	0	0	0	0	Prop-forward / hooker.
Rogerson, L.	18/1/1919	1/2/19	2	0	0	0	0	Centre / loose-forward.
Rollings, G.D.	26/9/25		1	0	0	0	0	Hooker. Made only appearance versus Barrow at home.
Rothwell, John	10/10/36	14/9/46	19	1	0	0	3	Forward from Barnes ARLFC. Sold to Rochdale Hornets.
Rudd, H.	1/12/23		1	0	0	0	0	Centre. Only appearance versus Leigh at Wilderspool.
Rutledge, Norman	30/9/33	2/5/36	15	2	0	0	6	Centre signed in May 1933. Transferred to Keighley.
Ryder, Freddie	25/8/23	17/11/28	156	41	10	1	145	Scrum-half and captain who later joined the coaching staff.
Rynn, J.	3/9/21		1	1	0	0	3	Centre. Try-scoring debut in 24-10 defeat at Barrow.
Scott, Bob	9/12/22	14/4/23	17	3	0	1	11	Cumbrian full-back signed from Aspatria. Sold to St Helens.
Seeling, Charlie	16/4/27	24/2/34	195	41	0	0	123	Club's top try-scoring loose-forward with 37. Sold to Wigan.
Shankland, Bill	29/8/31	15/4/38	231	74	70	0	362	Australian centre. Hall of Fame. Became top-class golfer
Siddall, Bill	25/8/23	25/4/25	35	11	10	0	53	Winger / stand-off.
Simcock, Fred	2/4/34	15/12/34	10	3	0	0	9	Winger signed from Castner Kellner RUFC. Sold to Widnes.
Skelhorn, Arthur	28/1/11	21/3/25	259	49	1	0	149	Versatile forward. 1920 tourist.
Skelhorn, J.R.	26/9/25		1	0	0	0	0	Loose-forward. Only game at home to Barrow.
Smith, Arthur	24/11/23	12/1/24	7	0	0	0	0	Centre from Cumbria. Debut in 35-0 defeat at Barrow.
Smith, Bob	28/1/33	27/10/34	53	6	0	0	18	Second row in 1933 Challenge Cup Final. Two caps for Lancashire.
Smith, Frank	15/2/19	11/9/20	18	1	0	0	3	Second-row forward. Only try versus Widnes at home.
Starkey, H.	1/1/34	29/12/34	2	0	0	0	0	Centre / full-back. Made debut at Rochdale Hornets.
Starkey, J.	8/12/23	19/4/24	3	0	0	0	0	Prop-forward.
Starkey, James	26/3/21	2/4/21	3	0	0	0	0	Centre.
Stevens, Charles	30/4/27		1	0	1	0	2	Stand-off at Oldham on last day of 1926-27 season.
Stockley, Bill	4/10/24	12/9/25	13	4	0	0	12	Winger. Scored hat-trick of tries on his Wire debut.
Storey, J.	18/2/28		1	0	0	0	0	Left winger in 11-10 victory versus Hunslet at home.
Stowell, Charlie	18/4/25		1	0	0	0	0	Centre signed from Warrington Rangers.
Talbot, William	10/2/23	21/4/23	12	3	0	0	9	Winger signed from Wigan & District ARL.
Taylor,	29/11/24		1	0	0	0	0	Prop-forward. Only game in 5-3 win at Salford.
Thompson, Tommy	1/10/27	30/3/34	202	112	14	0	364	Side-stepping winger. Nicknamed 'Tubby'. Hall of Fame.
Tranter, Jim	16/12/11	26/12/28	439	120	0	6	372	Centre / back row. Tough tackler.

Vowles, Bill	8/1/27	5/3/27	7	1	0	0	3	Right wing signed from Bradford in exchange for Ned Catterall.
Waldron, Tom	12/11/27	6/9/30	4	0	0	0	0	Half-back from local amateur RL. Transferred to Widnes.
Walker, George	13/9/19	30/10/26	65	13	2	0	43	Centre / second row featured in Pinnace cigarette cards.
Waywell, Jack	26/9/10	22/11/19	98	26	0	0	78	Winger. Leading try-scorer in 1913-14 season with nine.
Webb, Bob	17/11/34	23/11/35	12	0	0	0	0	Forward signed from Manchester Ship Canal ARLFC.
Welsby, Eric	3/3/34	30/8/39	104	8	0	1	26	Second row. Kicked drop-goal in 1937 Championship Final.
Wheatley, Stan	27/12/21	13/11/26	57	2	27	0	60	Stand-off. Product of Warrington's 'A' team.
Whitcombe, Harry	6/12/24	24/1/25	9	1	0	0	3	Forward signed from Nuneaton RUFC.
Wilcock, William	8/11/19	10/1/20	3	0	0	0	0	Winger.
Williams, Frank	12/11/21	24/2/34	352	87	0	0	261	Second row. Lancashire Cup winner in 1929.
Williams, John L.	7/9/29		1	0	0	0	0	Winger. Only game in heavy defeat at Swinton.
Wilmot, Tommy	11/3/22	4/9/22	6	1	0	0	3	Centre. Scored only try versus Salford at home.
Woodcock, H.	2/2/35	12/10/35	6	0	0	0	0	Hooker.
Woods, Jack	3/2/34	31/8/35	14	5	0	0	15	Winger signed from Barrow. Transferred to Liverpool Stanley.
Worsley, Jim	8/12/23	26/3/27	5	0	0	0	0	Forward.
Wright, A.	8/4/22	6/10/23	22	0	3	0	6	Full-back / centre featured in Pinnace cigarette cards.

229 players.
Competitive games only included, not friendlies.

What they said about Geoff Lee's previous Ashurst novels:

"I found it [*One Winter*] warm and authentic and an enjoyable read."
Stan Barstow (author of *A Kind of Loving*)

"Incredibly readable"
Wakefield Express

"Geoff Lee's prose envelopes the reader in a comforting warm glow of nostalgia. He has a sharp eye for characters and an even sharper ear for dialogue."
Yorkshire Evening Post

"Geoff has certainly developed his writing skills since we both shared a desk at Knowsley Road School. I thoroughly enjoyed his first two novels which both brought back many memories for me. They were well written, realistic and included some hilarious dialogue."
Ray French (*BBC Television rugby league commentator and journalist*)

Set in the fictional town of Ashurst in south Lancashire in the early 1960s, against the background of the worst winter in living memory, ***One Winter*** is a vivid and humorous account of working class life at home, work and play. ***One Autumn*** is the fourth novel about life in Ashurst. 1992 and 1993 were tough years. Did Wilkinson's survive the Dutch takeover? What happened to the town's railway station? Did the campaign to keep the library open succeed and did Thelma recover from her accident?

Published at £9.95, available for £9.00 for each book, post free, from London League Publications Ltd, PO Box 10441, London E14 8WR; credit card orders via our website: www.llpshop.co.uk or by phone on 0845-230-1895. The books can be ordered from any bookshop at full price.

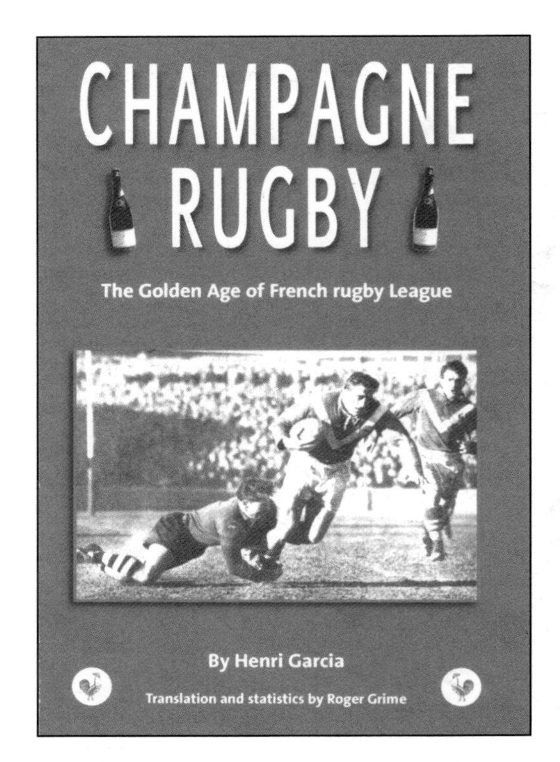

Champagne Rugby covers the 1950s was the Golden Age of French Rugby League. After being banned by the collaborative Vichy regime during the Second World War, the sport quickly rebuilt and in 1951 a French rugby league team toured Australia for the first time. Playing flowing, attacking rugby, they shocked the Australians with a decisive victory in the test series. Their famous full-back, Puig Aubert, broke the points scoring record for a tourist.

In 1955, France again defeated the Australians, and in 1960, with a squad hit by injuries, drew the test series. This book is the story of those famous tours and also gives a French viewpoint on the game's origins. First published in 1960, and produced here for the first time in English, it is a wonderful record of three great French teams. The author, Henri Garcia, was the rugby league correspondent of *L'Equipe*, and covered all three tours for that newspaper. All rugby league fans will enjoy this fascinating book.

Published at £12.95, available direct from London League Publications for £12.00.

Snuff out the Moon outlines the development of floodlit rugby league, from the early days of floodlit rugby in the 1870s to today.

This book, based on extensive original research, examines the developments in electricity that brought about those early matches and explains how they were organised. It then brings the story up to date and looks at the development of the use of floodlights in modern rugby league from the 1930s through the 1950s and the 1955 ITV Television Trophy to the use of floodlights today. The book also considers the relationship between rugby league and big business, and the issue of television coverage of the game.

Published at £11.95, available direct from London League Publications for £11.00.

Order from London League Publications Ltd, PO Box 10441, London E14 8WR;
credit card orders via our website: www.llpshop.co.uk or by phone on 0845-230-1895.
The books can be ordered from any bookshop at full price.

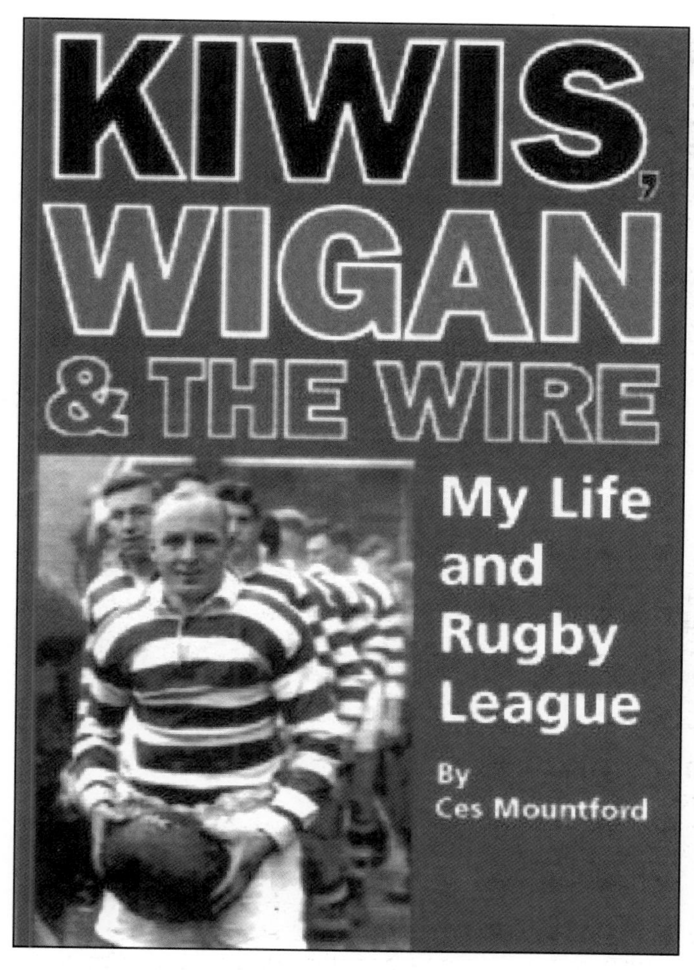

Ces Mountford is recognised as one of the greatest Kiwi Rugby League players of all time. He joined **Wigan** in 1946, and was a key member of the great post-war Wigan team. In 1951, he was the first foreign player to win the Lance Todd Trophy.

In 1951, he joined **Warrington** as manager and stayed with the club for 10 years, including some of their greatest triumphs, including the 1954 Cup and Championship Double. He then returned to New Zealand, and developed Rugby League coaching, including managing the national team.

He was awarded the MBE for his services to Rugby League. Now living in retirement in Australia, this book looks back on a fascinating life, including growing up on the West Coast of New Zealand and his experience in British rugby league. The book also includes contributions from many past players and colleagues. It is well illustrated with photographs and cartoons from his full Rugby League career.

Published at £9.95, now available direct from London League Publications at £5.00 post free. Order from London League Publications Ltd, PO Box 10441, London E14 8WR; credit card orders via our website: www.llpshop.co.uk or by phone on 0845-230-1895.
The book can be ordered from any bookshop at full price.

For a great selection of rugby league books, visit

www.llpshop.co.uk

Or write for a free catalogue / booklist to PO Box 10441, London E14 8WR

A Two Horse Town
50 years in broadcasting
Keith Macklin